Contents

STRAND 1
Who am I?

STRAND 3
Team Up

STRAND 1
Who am I?

STRAND 2
Minding Myself and Others

STRAND 2
Minding Myself and Others

STRAND 3
Team Up

STRAND 4
Mental Health and Wellbeing

STRAND 1
Who am I?

STRAND 2
Minding Myself and Others

STRAND 2
Minding Myself and Others

Preface

Welcome to *New Healthy Lifestyles*

This new edition retains all of the lessons required for teaching the existing modular course: simply follow the **Modular Course Overview** on page v to do so. It is also designed to fulfil the criteria for teaching SPHE as a **Short Course** for the new Junior Cycle: The contents list on page iii is structured around the topics and strands recommended for the new Short Course in SPHE.

The **Up for the Challenge** feature at the end of each topic allows students to apply what they have learned to real life situations. These challenges also prepare students for assessment related to the certification of the short course; see your **Teacher's Resource Book on gillmacmillan.ie** for more detail.

We have retained many of the favourite features of the highly popular first edition, such as crosswords and wordsearches. We have also added the following features, which means that, whatever approach your school is taking for SPHE, you will have an easy-to-follow and comprehensive set of lessons for your classes. These new features include:

- A ready-to-go, lesson-by-lesson approach
- A Teacher's Resource Book available on gillmacmillan.ie which gives practical guidelines on how to implement the material in the student books
- Links to websites which provide extra background information for the teacher and enhances the student's knowledge of a topic
- Each lesson is based on the experiential learning model which means that students will be actively engaged in their own learning
- Each lesson concludes with a **Learning Keepsake**, which ensures students maintain a personal learning journal as recommended by the NCCA.
- Exercises to improve students' literacy and numeracy skills are in-built
- An **eBook** version which contains many fun videos and animations to enhance lessons
- Extra lessons and exciting and interesting worksheets and articles in our Teacher's Resource Book.

New Healthy Lifestyles has received very positive reviews from SPHE teachers who have used it in class. They have found it fun, relevant and up to date and we hope you do too!

Edel O'Brien and Catherine Deegan

NEW

Healthy
Lifestyles 1

The Complete Package for Junior Cycle SPHE

Catherine Deegan & Edel O'Brien

GILL & MACMILLAN

Gill & Macmillan
Hume Avenue
Park West
Dublin 12
with associated companies throughout the world
www.gillmacmillan.ie

Design by Tanya M Ross Elementinc.ie
Illustrations by Derry Dillon

The paper used in this book is made from the wood pulp of managed forests. For every tree felled, at least one tree is planted, thereby renewing natural resources.

For permission to reproduce photographs, the authors and publisher gratefully acknowledge the following:

© Advertising Archive: 172CL; © Alamy: 3L, 80, 83C, 83R, 84CL, 99BL, 99TC, 106CTL, 112B, 123TL, 123TC, 123BC, 128C, 128CB, 135L, 148L, 159L, 159CL, 159R, 160CL, 160R, 163, 165, 172TL, 172CR, 172R, 177TR, 177TCL, 177CBR, 177BCL, 177BL, 177BR, 179; © Getty Images: 135R, 144TL, 177CTR; © Imagefile: 144TR; © Photocall Ireland: 26, 36; © Shutterstock: 1, 3TR, 3BR, 4, 7, 40, 49, 62, 72, 83L, 84TL, 84TR, 84CR, 84BL, 84BR, 95T, 95B, 97TCR, 97L, 97BR, 97TCL, 97TR, 97BL, 97BCR, 99TL, 99BR, 99TR, 106TL, 106TR, 106TCR, 106CL, 106CR, 106BCL, 106BCR, 106BL, 106BR, 110, 112T, 116, 123BL, 128T, 128CT, 128B, 132, 144CL, 144CBR, 144BL, 144BR, 145R, 145C, 146L, 148R, 159CR, 170, 177TL; © Shutterstock/fotostory: 21; © Shutterstock/Helga Esteb: 160TL; © Shutterstock/Rena Schild: 123BR; © Shutterstock/Ververidis Vasilis: 160CR.

The authors and publisher have made every effort to trace all copyright holders, but if any has been inadvertently overlooked we would be pleased to make the necessary arrangement at the first opportunity.

Modular Course Overview

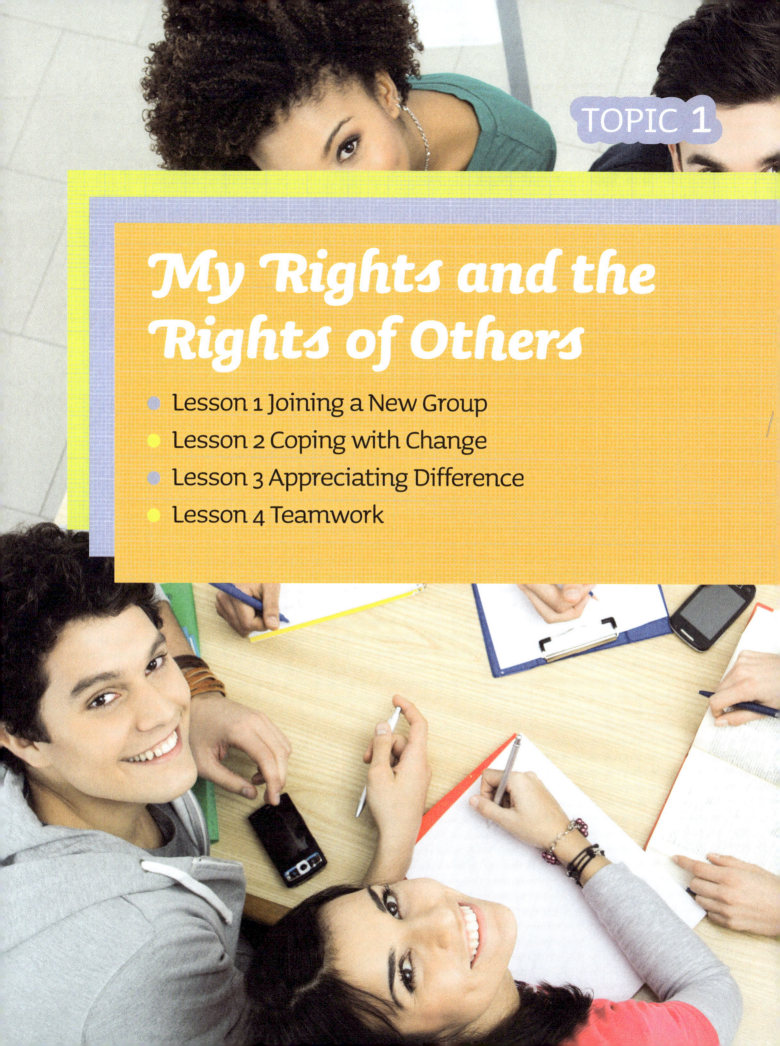

My Rights and the Rights of Others

LESSON 1
Joining a New Group

At the end of this lesson . . .
. . . you will have improved your group work and communication skills.

Key Words
- SPHE
- Communication
- Class contract
- Confidentiality

Keyskill
- Working with others

Welcome to your new SPHE class. SPHE stands for Social, Personal and Health Education. In SPHE you will learn about yourself, and about your relationships with others. In today's lesson you will get to know your classmates and you will agree a work contract with the ground rules for SPHE class.

Class Activity

- You have 15 minutes to walk around the classroom and meet as many students as possible and ask them a question.
- Fill in their answer and their name.
- When the time is up, return to your seat and read over the answers.
- Highlight any answers you really liked.
- Answer the questions that follow.

Name	Question	Answer
	If you could travel back in time, what period in history would you go back to?	
	What country would you really like to visit?	
	If you could watch any movie right now, what would it be?	
	What famous person in the world would you most like to spend a day with?	
	If you don't have a pet, what sort of pet would you like to have?	
	If you were an animal, which animal would you be?	
	What's your favourite thing to do in the summer?	
	What is your favourite day of the week?	
	If you were going to be marooned on a desert island, what three things would you bring?	
	If you won the lotto, what would you do with the money?	

	Who is your favourite cartoon character?	
	Were you named after someone special? If so, who?	
	What is your favourite television programme?	
	What is your favourite book?	
	What was the weirdest thing you have ever eaten?	
	How tall are you?	
	What was the hardest thing you have ever done?	
	Would you rather be the best-looking person or the smartest person?	
	If you were at your friend's house and you found an insect in your dinner, what would you do?	
	Do you prefer Italian food or Chinese food?	
	If you could change one thing in the world, what would it be?	
	Would you most like to be happy or rich or famous?	
	Can you sing or play a musical instrument?	
	Who is your hero and why?	
	What is the funniest thing that has ever happened to you?	
	Would you rather be too hungry or too cold?	
	Would you prefer to sleep in the top bunk or in the bottom bunk?	
	If you could change your first name, what name would you choose?	

Individual Activity

1. How many people did you speak to who you didn't already know?

    _____
    _____

2. Which question did you find the most interesting?

    _____
    _____

3. Which question did you find least interesting?

    _____
    _____

4. What was the easiest thing about this activity?

    _____
    _____

5. What was the hardest thing about this activity?

    _____
    _____

6. Did you get to speak to everyone in the class? If not, why not?

    _____
    _____

7. If you were doing this activity again, what would you do differently and why?

    _____
    _____

Confidentiality

Most of the questions in the questionnaire are not really serious and it can be fun to listen to the answers that everyone gives. But sometimes in SPHE class, sensitive subjects can arise. Confidentiality means respecting your own privacy and the privacy of others.

Some things are not suitable for revealing in class. If you feel concerned or sensitive about certain things, it is important that you find a trusted adult to talk to. Confidentiality also means that if someone reveals something personal in class it should not be spoken about outside class.

Group Activity

Confidentiality is one of the most important ground rules for SPHE. Other important ground rules include:

1. Listen when others are speaking.
2. Respect other people's opinions even if they are different from your own.

Two examples have been given. Write down any other ground rules your group considers important for SPHE class to work well.

-
-
-
-
-

Class Activity

Choose a reporter from your group to share your group's ideas with the rest of the class. The class as a whole must now try to agree to a set of ground rules. When the whole class has agreed on these ground rules, write them into the contract opposite. Ensure each ground rule begins with an 'I' statement, e.g. 'I will listen when others are speaking.' When you have written your agreed ground rules everyone must sign the contract to show that they agree.

CLASS CONTRACT

Learning **Keepsake**

Three things I have learned about my SPHE class are:

1. _____
2. _____
3. _____

As a result of what I have learned about joining a new group, I will:

_____

_____

_____

_____ has shared this Learning Keepsake with me _____

Name of student   Parent's/guardian's signature

LESSON 2
Coping with Change

At the end of this lesson . . .

. . . you will have identified ways of coping in your new school.

Key Words
- Change
- Anxiety
- Solution
- Roles

Keyskill
- Staying well

A new school brings with it a lot of changes: new teachers, new subjects, a new timetable, new classmates and a new school building. You may be feeling nervous about what lies ahead. This is all very natural. The following exercise is designed to help you cope with the exciting changes you will come across as you settle in to your new school.

Group Activity

Below are examples of some problems students may encounter when starting secondary school. In your group, write down solutions to each problem.

What could you do if . . .?

You left your lunch at home

_____
_____

You misplaced your tie after PE

_____

You have yet to make any real friends

_____

Your homework is taking a long time

_____
_____

You cannot understand something the teacher is explaining

_____
_____

A person in your year starts making insulting remarks to you

_____
_____

You forgot your journal

_____
_____

Individual Activity

Which problem was the easiest to find a solution to?

_____

_____

Which problem was the most difficult to find a solution to?

_____

_____

Did anyone in your group actually have any of these problems? If so, what did they do?

_____

_____

Finding important people and places in our school

Individual Activity

In the table below, write the names, roles and locations of adults who can help you in your school. Under 'Location', give the room number and say where it is in the school.

People who help

Title	Name	Role	Location
Principal			
Deputy Principal			
Year Head			
Class Tutor			
Secretary			
Caretaker			
Chaplain			
Guidance Counsellor			
Shop Keeper			

Individual Activity

Now that you have identified the important people and places in your school, write down your subjects, your teachers and the numbers and locations of the rooms that you are in.

My subjects and teachers

Subject	Teacher	Location

Write down five things that are different between primary and secondary school.

	Primary	Secondary
1		
2		
3		
4		
5		

Which change do you find most difficult? Why?

_____

_____

_____

_____

Can you think of any other difficulties that you might experience as a first year student? Name the difficulty and suggest how it could be resolved.
Which changes do you really enjoy? Why?

Difficulty	Solution

Write your favourite thing about secondary school in the smiley face.

Learning *Keepsake*

Three things I have learned about my new school are:

1. _____
2. _____
3. _____

As a result of what I have learned about coping with change, I will:

_____
_____
_____

_____ has shared this Learning Keepsake with me _____
Name of student   Parent's/guardian's signature

LESSON 3
Appreciating Difference

At the end of this lesson . . .

. . . you will appreciate your own individuality and talents and the individuality and talents of others in your class.

Key Words
- Difference
- Achievements
- Talent
- Unique
- Inclusive

Keyskill
- Working with others

Everyone in the class is different. It is good for us to recognise our own unique personality and talents while also appreciating the uniqueness and talents of those around us.

 Individual Activity

On a large poster page, draw the picture frame below. In each frame draw, write in or stick in pictures of your unique qualities or talents.

I like

I am good at

My hopes are

My favourite subject is

My achievements are

The talent I admire most in someone else is

I am a good friend because

Group Activity

In your groups discuss the picture frames. Write your answers below.

The most surprising talent in our group is _____

The number of people in our group who share the same talents is _____

From our picture frames the talents that are in this group are:

_____

Group Activity

Some people get singled out or excluded. Give three reasons why you think this happens.

1. _____
2. _____
3. _____

Suggest three ways in which your class could be more inclusive.

1. _____
2. _____
3. _____

Class Activity

Put a picture of yourself in the frame. Everyone in the class must write a compliment about you around the frame.

Suggest three ways you could make others feel good about themselves.

1. _____

2. _____

3. _____

Learning *Keepsake*

Three things I have learned about people in my class are:

1. _____
2. _____
3. _____

As a result of what I have learned about appreciating difference, I will:

_____
_____
_____

_____ has shared this Learning Keepsake with me _____
Name of student   Parent's/guardian's signature

LESSON 4
Teamwork

At the end of this lesson . . .
. . . you will understand the importance of teamwork
. . . and you will know how to be a good team player.

Key Words
- Teamwork
- Roles
- Decisions

Keyskill
- Working with others

Who would you save?

There has been a huge earthquake and a large community has been buried under rubble. The rescue services arrive and they know that there are ten people still alive trapped under a collapsed hospital. They have limited resources and time is running out. They know that they can definitely save four people.

These are the ten people who are still alive:

1. A twelve-year-old boy who is a straight A student.
2. A seventy-year-old female smoker with a serious lung condition.
3. A twenty-five-year-old male who is a small-time criminal.
4. A female doctor whose husband is seriously ill and who has three young children.
5. A male charity worker who has raised lots of money for cancer research.
6. A female nurse who is due to retire next month.
7. A professional soccer player who has just got a contract with a major club.
8. A young boy aged eight who is disabled.
9. A male prison warden who was bringing a criminal to hospital for medical tests.
10. A young woman who is four months pregnant.

Individual Activity

You are a member of the rescue team. You have five minutes to pick four people from the list to be rescued and give reasons for your answer.

Survivor A: _____

Why? _____

_____

Survivor B: _____

Why? _____

_____

Survivor C: _____

Why? _____

_____

Survivor D: _____

Why? _____

_____

Group Activity

Now that you have decided who you would save, take fifteen minutes to work in your group to come to an agreement about which four people you all will save.

Assign the following roles to the members of your group.

Role	Responsibility
Chairperson	Ensures the group remains focused on the task Ensures that everyone has an opportunity to speak
Timekeeper	Keeps the time and reminds the chairperson how much time is left
Reporter	Takes notes and reports back to the class
Observer	Watches what is happening in the group Notes what is helpful in getting the task finished and what prevents this from happening

Survivor A: _____

Survivor B: _____

Survivor C: _____

Survivor D: _____

Class Activity

1. How did you make your decisions individually?
2. How did your group make its decisions?
3. What were the challenges? How did you handle disagreement?
4. Was there a leader in your group?
5. Who decided on the leader?
6. Did everyone get an opportunity to talk?
7. What helped you to reach your decision?
8. What was unhelpful?
9. What might you do differently if you were to do the task again?

Roles in groups

In the last activity you learned about roles that are helpful when people are working in groups or teams. Here are some other roles that people often take when working as part of a group or team.

1. **Leader:** Takes control of the task and tries to organise others.
2. **Followers:** Does not try to control the task but is happy to participate and follow instructions.
3. **Boat-rocker:** Disagrees with the group and often has strongly held opinions and ideas which they are slow to change.

4. **Peacemaker:** Offers support and tries to create agreement in the group.
5. **Joker:** Deliberately tries to disrupt the activity and distracts people around them.

Individual Activity

Record your own and others' helpful and unhelpful behaviours in the grid below.

What I did that helped the group	What I did that hindered the group
What other people did that helped the group	What other people did that hindered the group

Learning *Keepsake*

Three things I learned about group work/teamwork are:

1. _____
2. _____
3. _____

As a result of what I have learned about working together, I will:

_____
_____
_____

_____ has shared this Learning Keepsake with me _____

Name of student   Parent's/guardian's signature

Topic Review

Date / /

In this topic I learned about

_____

This topic is useful to me in my life because

_____

_____

In this topic I liked

_____

_____

In this topic I did not like

_____

_____

I would like to find out more about

_____

_____

Key Skills I have used in this topic are:

- ☐ Managing myself
- ☐ Staying well
- ☐ Communicating
- ☐ Being creative
- ☐ Working with others
- ☐ Managing information and thinking

*Are you up for the challenge?
Design an activity that will help develop team building skills in you class.

Anti-Bullying

LESSON 5

Bullying is Everyone's Business

At the end of this lesson . . .

. . . you will understand what bullying is

. . . and you will be able to identify different types of bullying behaviour.

Key Words
- Intimidating
- Humiliating
- Cyber bullying

Keyskill
- Staying safe

Bullying behaviour
Understanding what bullying is and identifying different types of bullying behaviour can help you to feel safe and happy at school.

Individual Activity

Write down six words related to bullying, e.g. pushing, threatening, ignoring . . .

1. _____
2. _____
3. _____
4. _____
5. _____
6. _____

Bo the Bully

Group Activity

In groups of four, put all your words together. Use all the words you wrote down to create your own poem. The first letter of each line of your poem must spell out the word 'bullying'. Use the sample below to help you. When you have finished make a large poster of your poem to display on the classroom wall

Bullying

Beating people up
Under pressure from others
Loves attention
Loneliness, all by myself
You never know when to stop
Insecure wherever I go
Need help
Getting out of control

Your group's poem

B
U
L
L
Y
I
N
G

Individual Activity

1. Using the words and your group's poem, finish the following sentence:
   Bullying is

   _____

   _____

   _____

2. From the words your group has chosen, write down the three most dangerous types of bullying behaviour.

   a) _____

   b) _____

   c) _____

3. Do you think that bullying behaviour is ever acceptable? Give reasons for your answer.

   _____

   _____

4. Do you think that boys and girls bully in different ways? Give reasons for your answer.

   _____

   _____

   _____

Forms of bullying

Now that you understand what bullying behaviour is, pair up each picture below with the matching form of bullying.

Each type of bullying involves hurtful and damaging behaviour.

A    **B**    **C**    **D**    **E**

1. Emotional/ social bullying
– ignoring, excluding, making threats and/or spreading rumours about another person.

2. Cyber bullying
– being unkind or threatening another person by phone, text and/or the internet.

3. Non-verbal bullying – making intimidating gestures and/or faces at another person.

4. Verbal bullying – name calling, teasing, insulting or embarrassing another person.

5. Physical bullying
– pushing, shoving, hitting, and/or kicking another person.

A	
B	
C	
D	
E	

Individual Activity

Banter and having a laugh can be good fun, but sometimes what you think is funny can hurt or upset another person. Remember, it's only fun if the other person sees it that way. Answer the following questions and try to reflect on your own behaviour.

Could you be a bully?

- Have you ever hurt or embarrassed someone on purpose?
- Have you ever picked on someone younger than you?
- Have you ever spread rumours about another person even though you knew they were not true?
- Have you ever tried to turn your friends against someone?
- Have you ever witnessed someone being bullied and not done anything to help?
- Have you ever used the excuse that you were only messing even though you knew you had hurt the other person's feelings?

Learning Keepsake

Three things I have learned about bullying are:

1. _____
2. _____
3. _____

As a result of what I have learned about bullying, I will:

_____
_____
_____

_____ has shared this Learning Keepsake with me _____
Name of student   Parent's/guardian's signature

LESSON 6
Dealing with Bullying: What Can You Do?

At the end of this lesson . . .
. . . you will know how to deal with bullying behaviour towards you or another person . . . and you will be familiar with your school's policy on bullying.

Key Words
- Policy
- Strategies
- Bystander

Keyskill
- Working with Others

Bullying Scenarios

Laura's Story

John and his friends are sitting on steps outside the local shop on a Saturday evening. They see Laura, a girl from school, coming out of the shop. Laura is a well-liked girl but she is not one of the 'cool group'. John has heard that she fancies his best friend Mark. John has a great idea for a laugh. He asks his friends if anyone has Laura's mobile number. Luke has it because he is in the same athletics club as Laura.

John texts Laura, pretending to be Mark. 'Hi Laura, Mark here, What's up?' Laura replies, 'Not much, just hanging around at home being a bit bored.' John texts back, 'I really like you and I'd love to go out with you.' Laura is delighted and texts back, 'I really like you too. When would you like to meet?'

John doesn't respond but he forwards the texts to all of the lads and some of the girls from school.

On Monday when Laura goes to school, she sees some of the girls in her class talking about her and laughing. Laura's friend Jean tells Laura about the text and says that she got it from John on Saturday night. Jean also says that some people are even laughing about it on Facebook. When Laura goes back to class someone has written on the board, 'Laura is a wannabe!' When the teacher comes in she gives Laura a sympathetic smile and wipes the board.

Individual Activity

1. How do you think Laura feels?

_____
_____
_____

2. What is the main type of bullying Laura experiences?

_____
_____
_____

3. Why do you think this type of bullying happens to young people?

_____
_____
_____

4. Could any bystanders have helped Laura? Explain your answer.

_____
_____
_____

The Football Game

Danny is in first year in school; he is very outspoken and often speaks out of turn in class. Danny doesn't mean to be cheeky, but he is very interested in lots of different subjects and likes to discuss things with his teachers. Lately, Danny has noticed that some of the other students start sniggering when he talks. In particular, two boys from Danny's primary school, Pat and Jim, make fun of Danny whenever he says anything.

Danny is quite good at soccer, and he plays with the school soccer team. One day after losing a match Danny and the rest of the team are getting changed in the changing rooms. Jim and Pat are on the team and they are not happy that they lost. They blame Danny for losing the match, saying that he did not mark his man properly. Danny tries to ignore them and continues to get changed. Pat shouts that they will never win with a gay person on the team. He goes over to Danny and pushes him. Danny falls backwards and lands on the floor and Pat starts to kick him. Everyone else in the dressing room starts to shout 'Fight, fight, fight!' and some of the team take out their phones and video the fight.

Eventually the coach comes in and stops the violence; he tries to find out what happened but no one is willing to tell him. The school is holding an investigation into what happened. Meanwhile, Danny can't face his team again.

Individual Activity

1. List the different forms of bullying that Danny is experiencing.

   _____

   _____

   _____

2. How do you think Danny is feeling?

   _____

   _____

   _____

3. Who could have helped Danny:

   a) in class? _____

   b) in the changing room? _____

4. What advice would you give to Danny?

   _____

   _____

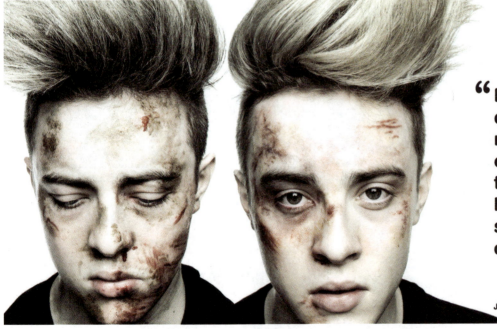

ISPCC
ALWAYS HERE FOR CHILDREN

" **Imagine if every child knew that nothing can ever happen that can't be fixed by someone who cares.** "

JOIN THE FIGHT FOR CHILDREN'S RIGHTS.
ISPCC.IE

How to deal with bullying

It can be difficult to deal with bullying behaviour, but here are some tips that can help you if you or someone else is being bullied. Remember, if you are being bullied *it is not your fault*. And if you are a bystander you can help stop the bullying.

What to do if you are being bullied

- Tell yourself that you do not deserve to be treated this way and that it is wrong.
- Try to ignore the behaviour and try not to show that you are upset. This is hard, but bullies thrive on other people's fear.
- Try not to fight back or use violence – this can make things worse.
- Try to use humour to lighten the mood.
- Get support from your friends and try not to become isolated.
- Keep a diary of when you have been bullied.
- If the behaviour continues or gets worse, tell someone you trust.

What to do if you are a bystander

- Discourage the bully by not joining in.
- Defend the victim.
- Try to distract people from the bullying behaviour.
- Get support from other students to stand up to the bully.
- Report the bullying to an adult whom you trust.
- Be a friend to someone who you feel is getting a hard time.

 Group Activity: Raising awareness in school

Look at your school's anti-bullying policy. Create anti-bullying slogans outlining what you and your school can do to prevent bullying. Post your slogans around your school.

Learning *Keepsake*

Three things I have learned about dealing with bullying are:

1. _____
2. _____
3. _____

As a result of what I have learned about anti-bullying, I will:

_____
_____
_____

_____ has shared this Learning Keepsake with me _____

Name of student   Parent's/guardian's signature

Topic Review

Date / /

In this topic I learned about
_____

This topic is useful to me in my life because
_____
_____

In this topic I liked
_____
_____

In this topic I did not like
_____
_____

I would like to find out more about
_____
_____

Key Skills I have used in this topic are:

☐ Managing myself
☐ Staying well
☐ Communicating
☐ Being creative
☐ Working with others
☐ Managing information and thinking

*Are you up for the challenge?

As a class, design and organise an anti-bullying week for your school to raise awareness about bullying.

TOPIC 3

Self-Management

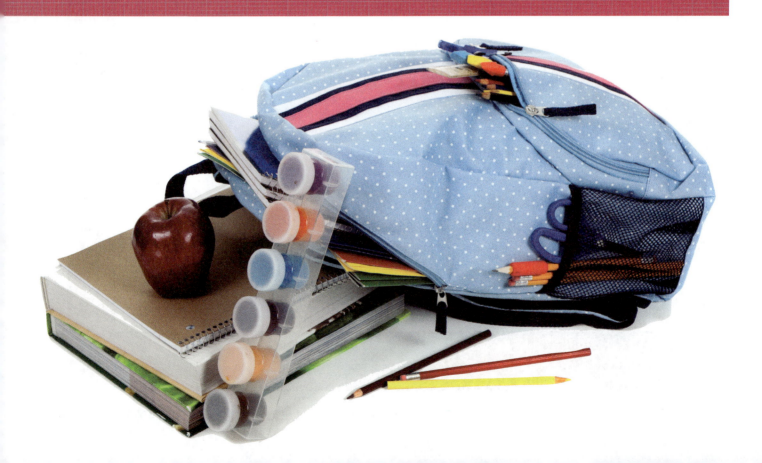

LESSON 7
Coping with Loss

At the end of this lesson . . .
. . . you will know the different types of loss that happen in people's lives
. . . and you will understand how to help people to cope with loss.

Key Words
- Change
- Grief
- Bereavement
- Loss

Keyskill
- Communicating

Harry is born.

Harry starts primary school.
He is frightened and lonely.

Harry makes friends
with Charlie. Harry is
very pleased as Charlie
is very nice. (They are
still friends today.)

Change is a natural part of life; and change can bring loss. However, with the support of friends and family a person can cope with the challenges that come with loss.

Meet Harry. He is fourteen years old. Look at the losses that have occurred in his life and his feelings about each one.

Brainstorm different losses young people might experience.

Harry's sister is born and
he is excited and jealous.

Harry's dad dies. Harry is heartbroken.

Harry moves house and he is sad and excited.

Harry's Timeline

Mum meets Pat. Pat is good fun.

Mum marries Pat. Harry is happy.

Harry breaks his leg. He is hurt and disappointed because he can't play in the school final.

Harry goes to secondary school and is feeling very nervous.

1. What change/loss do you think Harry found the most difficult? Give reasons for your answer.

_____

_____

_____

2. Who or what could have helped Harry to cope with the changes and losses in his life?

_____

_____

_____

3. What advice would you give to Harry as he starts secondary school?

_____

_____

_____

Group Activity

As you can see, Harry has experienced many changes and some losses in his life. This is similar to other people his age. Suggest ways in which you could support a young person who has experienced a loss. The first two suggestions have been written in for you.

Do	Don't
Say you are sorry about what happened	Avoid them because you feel awkward
_____	_____
_____	_____
_____	_____
_____	_____
_____	_____
_____	_____

Your Timeline

Individual Activity

Fill in your timeline with the changes and losses that have occurred in your life.

In the space below, write the things that helped you to cope with these changes and losses.

REMEMBER! Only include things that you are comfortable talking about.

Things that help me cope

Learning *Keepsake*

Three things I have learned about loss and bereavement are:

1. _____
2. _____
3. _____

As a result of what I have learned about coping with loss, I will:

_____
_____
_____

_____ has shared this Learning Keepsake with me _____
Name of student   Parent's/guardian's signature

LESSON 8
Organising Myself

At the end of this lesson . . .
. . . you will be able to organise your homework and school life

Key Words
- Preparation
- Timetable
- Organise

 # Keyskill
- Managing myself

Getting organised

Now that you are in secondary school you have a lot more subjects and a lot more to remember. A few minutes spent preparing yourself every night or even at break times can help you to feel more organised and relaxed about your day.

Complete the questionnaire below to find out just how organised (or not) you are.

Individual Activity

How organised am I?

1. I am on time for school:

   a) Always
   b) Sometimes
   c) Never

2. My locker is tidy:

   a) Always
   b) Sometimes
   c) Never

3. I write all my homework, both written and oral, into my homework journal:

   a) Always
   b) Sometimes
   c) Never

4. I check my timetable every night to make sure I have everything I need for the next day:
   a) Always
   b) Sometimes
   c) Never

5. I leave homework and projects until the last minute:

   a) Always
   b) Sometimes
   c) Never

6. I organise my hand-outs and put them in a folder when I get them:
   a) Always
   b) Sometimes
   c) Never

7. I can read my own notes and my own handwriting:

a) Always

b) Sometimes

c) Never

8. I give school notices to my parents/guardians on time:

a) Always

b) Sometimes

c) Never

9. I have to ask permission to go to my locker during class to get books or materials I have forgotten.

a) Never

b) Sometimes

c) Always

10. I can find my tie and other clothes I need in the mornings:

a) Always

b) Sometimes

c) Never

With help from your teacher, fill in your scores in the grid below.

For each (a) score 10 points; for each (b) score 5; for each (c) score 0.

Question	a/b/c	Score
1		
2		
3		
4		
5		
6		
7		
8		
9		
10		

Interpreting your score

0–40 You need to work on your organisation skills. Your school journal and your timetable can help you to do this.

45–75 Your organisation skills are quite good. Identify the areas that you can improve and work on them.

80–100 You have excellent organisation skills. Keep up the good work.

Getting more organised

Group Activity

In your group, discuss the answers to the following questions. Fill in the answers in the space provided.

1. How can you ensure that you arrive to school/class on time?

2. What can you do to help you remember all your books and materials for each day?

3. What must you do to have all homework completed on time?

4. In order to arrive to school looking tidy and well presented, what must you do each day?

Individual Activity

My Personal Timetable

Using your school journal timetable, fill in what you need to bring to school each day.

Monday	Tuesday	Wednesday	Thursday	Friday	Everyday

SCHOOL JOURNAL

Name
School
Grade

Learning *Keepsake*

Three things I have learned about getting organised are:

1. _____
2. _____
3. _____

As a result of what I have learned about being organised, I will:

_____
_____
_____

_____ has shared this Learning Keepsake with me _____

Name of student   Parent's/guardian's signature

LESSON 9

Organising My Work at Home and at School

At the end of this lesson . . .
. . . you will know how to plan your study time efficiently.

Key Words
- Commitments
- Schedule

Keyskill
- Managing myself

Organising Orla

Orla is a first-year student. She has decided to draw up a study timetable for the year. She has a busy social life and enjoys her leisure time with friends and family. Orla's day usually begins around 7.45 and she leaves the house at 8.30 to walk to school.

School finishes at 3.50 every day. Orla has camogie training on Monday and Wednesday afternoons from 4 p.m. until 5 p.m.

Orla usually walks home from school. Dinner is usually ready at 6 p.m. Orla and her sister must tidy the kitchen after dinner on weeknights; they have usually finished clearing up by 7 p.m. Orla's favourite TV programmes are on from 7.30 to 8.30 on Tuesdays and Thursdays. Orla usually tries to get her homework done before dinner every evening, but if this isn't possible she usually spends an hour before bedtime on it. She sometimes does her homework in front of the TV. She is in bed by 10.30 most nights.

On Fridays Orla walks home with her friends from school, arriving home at 5 p.m. Normally she goes to the local swimming pool from 6 p.m. to 7.30. After her dinner on a Friday Orla usually spends a few hours babysitting next door.

Saturday is her favourite day. She stays in bed until about 11 a.m. and then she either goes training or plays a match until about 1.30 p.m. In the afternoon she usually tidies her room or bakes with her mother and on Saturday evening she often goes to the cinema with her friends. Sunday is always spent lazing around or vising her Nan and by Sunday afternoon she is exhausted and in no mood to study.

TIME	MONDAY	TUESDAY	WEDNESDAY	THURSDAY	FRIDAY
9.00	English	Home Economics	English	Tech Graphics	Maths
9.40	Irish	Home Economics	History	Tech Graphics	History
10.20	Geography	Tech Graphics	Science	Maths	Tech Graphics
11.00					
11.15	Science	Irish	Maths	Irish	Info Technology
11.55	Spanish	Spanish	Maths	English	English
12.30	Religious Education	Religious Education	Religious Education	Science	Home Economics
13.10					
13.50	Maths	History	SPHE	Spanish	Science
14.30	PE	English	Geography	Geography	CSPE
15.10	PE	Maths	Irish	Home Economics	Spanish

Group Activity

Based on what you know about Orla, answer the following questions.

1. What commitments does Orla have to take into account before she draws up her study timetable?

_____

_____

2. What changes could Orla make to her study area to make her study time more effective? Give reasons for your answer.

_____

_____

3. What is the best time for Orla to begin her homework each day? Give reasons for your answer.

_____

_____

_____

Monday: _____

_____

_____

Tuesday: _____

_____

_____

Wednesday: _____

_____

_____

Thursday: _____

_____

_____

Friday/Saturday/Sunday: _____

_____

_____

4. If Orla has a test in Home Economics for her double class on Tuesday morning, when could she fit in some extra study time?

_____

5. What are the things Orla could change in order to give herself more time to study?

_____

_____

Good study habits

Here are some ways of improving your study habits. Remember that doing your homework well is a very good way of studying.

1. Keep your study area tidy and organised.
2. Make sure you have all the materials and books you need before you begin.
3. Switch off your mobile phone and all other distractions before you begin.
4. Do your homework in the same place every night.
5. Do your homework at a designated time each night to set up a good routine.
6. Do both written and oral homework. If you have no homework in a subject, read over what you did in class that day.
7. Tick off your homework in your homework journal as you do it.
8. Do not spend more than an hour and a half on your homework in first year.
9. If you have an important test coming up, make sure that you have allowed enough time in your study timetable to fit in extra work.
10. If you are stuck on a question, ask someone at home for help. Do not spend the entire evening trying to work it out.

Now look at your own week and answer the following questions.

1. What commitments do you have to take into account before you draw up your homework/study timetable?

   _____

   _____

2. What changes could you make to where and how you study to make your study time more effective?

   _____

   _____

3. What is the best time for you to begin your homework each day? Give reasons for your answer.

   _____

   _____

   Monday   _____

   Tuesday   _____

   Wednesday _____

   Thursday   _____

   Friday   _____

4. What things could you change to give yourself more time to study?

   _____

   _____

Learning *Keepsake*

Three things I have learned about good study habits are:

1. _____

2. _____

3. _____

As a result of what I have learned about creating a study timetable, I will:

_____

_____

_____

_____ has shared this Learning Keepsake with me _____

Name of student   Parent's/guardian's signature

LESSON 10
Balance in My Life

At the end of this lesson . . .
. . . you will have reflected on what it means to be healthy
. . . and you will have explored the importance of balance in your life.

Key Words
- Balance
- Lifestyle
- Wellbeing

 # Keyskill
- Managing Myself

'All work and no play makes Jack a dull boy.' This is an old saying, but it does make sense. Remember, being healthy means having a healthy mind as well as a healthy body.

Group Activity

Select ten statements that you think best describe what it means to be healthy. In the table below rank them in order of importance from 1 to 10. For each statement, tick which column you think is the area of health your statement applies to. An example has been done for you.

A healthy person is someone who . . .	Physical	Mental	Social
Has a healthy diet?	✔		
1.			
2.			
3.			
4.			
5.			
6.			
7.			
8.			
9.			
10.			

Class Activity

What does your group think was the most important statement about good health? Give reasons for your answer.

The World Health Organisation (WHO) defines health as a state of complete physical, mental and social wellbeing, and not merely the absence of disease or infirmity.
In order to be healthy and lead a balanced life it is important to manage your time properly between school work, relaxation, leisure time and sleep.

Finding balance in our lives

Individual Activity

You can find balance in your life by taking care of yourself and managing your time well. In first year, for example, you have to spend a lot of time on school work, but if you devote too much time to school work and not enough time to exercise and having fun, your life can become out of balance.

In the table below write down how much time you spend on each activity on a typical day. Colour these times into the 24-hour clock below.

Sleeping	School, homework, study	Meeting friends	Excercise	Relaxing	Eating	TV, social networks, video games	Other

What can you start doing to ensure that there is more balance in your life? What do you need to stop doing to gain more balance in your life?

What I can start doing to gain more balance in my life	What I need to stop doing to gain more balance in my life

Learning *Keepsake*

Three things I learned about being healthy are:

1. _____
2. _____
3. _____

As a result of what I have learned about finding balance in my life, I will:

_____
_____
_____

_____ has shared this Learning Keepsake with me _____

Name of student   Parent's/guardian's signature

Topic Review

Date / /

In this topic I learned about

_____

This topic is useful to me in my life because

_____

_____

In this topic I liked

_____

_____

In this topic I did not like

_____

_____

I would like to find out more about

_____

_____

Key Skills I have used in this topic are:

- ☐ Managing myself
- ☐ Staying well
- ☐ Communicating
- ☐ Being creative
- ☐ Working with others
- ☐ Managing information and thinking

*Are you up for the challenge?

Create an easy to read booklet that provides advice on starting secondary school. You can include such things as getting organised, study and homework tips.

TOPIC 4

Respectful Communication

LESSON 11
Express Yourself

At the end of this lesson . . .
. . . you will understand how words, body language and tone come together to help you to express yourself.

Key Words
- Body language
- Tone
- Verbal communication
- Appropriate

Keyskill
- Communicating

How do we communicate?

53% = body language

40% = tone

7% = verbal

Young people sometimes find it difficult to express their feelings and opinions. If you do not clearly express what you think or feel, people can misunderstand you.

It is useful to practise what you want to say before you say it. This can help you to choose the right words for a particular situation.

It is also important to remember that only 7 per cent of communication is contained in the words we use. The rest comes from body language and tone of voice. For example, many words, phrases and sentences have a different meaning depending on the tone in which they are said and the words that are stressed.

Pair Activity

Practise saying the following sentence in three different tones:
- I had a great day (sarcastic)
- I had a great day (happy)
- I had a great day (surprised)

Now pick other statements and try changing the tone in which you say them.

Individual Activity

Look at each of the pictures below and write down what you think the body language is saying. Write down whether or not you think the body language is appropriate and say why or why not.

Picture 1

What is the body language saying?

_____

_____

_____

_____

Is it appropriate?_____

Why/why not?_____

_____

_____

Picture 2

What is the body language saying?

_____

_____

_____

_____

Is it appropriate? _____

Why/why not?_____

_____

_____

Picture 3

What is the body language saying?

_____

_____

_____

_____

Is it appropriate? _____

Why/why not?_____

_____

_____

Picture 4

What is the body language saying?

_____

_____

_____

_____

Is it appropriate? _____

Why/why not?_____

_____

_____

Picture 5

What is the body language saying?

_____

_____

_____

_____

Is it appropriate? _____

Why/why not?_____

_____

_____

Picture 6

What is the body language saying?

_____

_____

_____

_____

Is it appropriate? _____

Why/why not?_____

_____

_____

Class Activity

1. Compare your answers with the rest of the class.
2. Were there any examples where you thought the body language was negative and your classmates disagreed with you?
3. Try to come up with other examples of body language and what they mean (e.g. pointing at another person can mean that you are being bossy towards them).

_____

_____

Three important things to remember when expressing yourself:

1. Choose your words carefully: although they are not the whole story they are important.
2. Be aware of your body language: is it sending out the right message?
3. Take care with your tone: be aware of how you say what you say.

Individual Activity

Answer the following questions.

What tone of voice and body language might you use if you were:

Annoyed?

_____

Bored ?

_____

Excited?

_____

Angry?

_____

Worried?

_____

Happy?

_____

Learning *Keepsake*

Three things I have learned about expressing myself are:

1. _____
2. _____
3. _____

As a result of what I have learned about communication, I will:

_____

_____

_____

_____ has shared this Learning Keepsake with me _____

Name of student   Parent's/guardian's signature

LESSON 12
Learning to Listen

At the end of this lesson . . .
. . . you will have learned and practised your listening skills
. . . and you will recognise the importance of being sensitive to others.

Key Words
- Listening
- Selective listening

Keyskill
- Communicating

Role Play

Martin and Ivan are friends. Martin meets Ivan on his own after school.

Martin	(upbeat) Hi, Ivan, how are things? (texting on his phone)
Ivan	(downbeat) All right.
Martin	(accusing) What is up with you? Your face could stop a clock.
Ivan	(defeated) I never got picked for the team.
Martin	(excited) Oh, actually, did I tell you I was made captain? I can't wait for the game. I think we've a very strong chance this year. (looking up from texting)
Ivan	(angry) Yeah, well it won't mean anything to me because I won't be on the team.
Martin	(smiling) Yeah, oh … uh, that is a bit of a bummer.
Ivan	To make things worse I was meant to go to Old Trafford next month for my birthday, but Dad has lost his job and now we can't afford to go.
Martin	Talking of trips, I can't wait to go on the outdoor pursuits trip with school.
Ivan	I'm not going. I couldn't ask them for money for trips like that at home.
Martin	You're joking! All the lads are going. Try to get around them – it will be a great trip. I'll be putting the pictures on Facebook so you can see all the craic if you can't go.
Ivan	Talk to you later.
Martin	Hope you cheer up before then.

Pair Activity

1. Describe how you think each of the characters in the dialogue were feeling as they walked home from school.

Martin:_____

_____

Ivan:_____

_____

2. Do you think the characters in the dialogue listened to each other? Why do you think that?

_____

_____

3. Give examples of poor listening skills in the dialogue.

_____

_____

_____

4. What could each character have done to show that they were listening?

_____

_____

_____

Class Activity

Discuss your answers with the rest of your class.

Five poor listening styles

Spacing out – this is when someone is talking to you and your mind starts to wander. You are caught up in your own thoughts.

2 Pretend listening – when you pretend you are paying attention by using sympathetic words/sounds such as 'yeah', 'uh huh', 'I know'.

3 Selective listening – when you only pay attention to the part of the conversation that you are interested in.

4 Word listening – you do not pick up the clues about how the person is feeling. You do not notice the other person's body language or tone of voice.

5 Self-centred listening – you're waiting for the other person to finish talking so that you can speak. You are more interested in telling your story than hearing what they have to say.

How to be a good listener

Listening is a skill, and you can learn how to become a good listener.

1. Be alert – pay attention to their words, their gestures and their tone of voice to fully understand how they are feeling.
2. Give the person your full attention – look straight at them, use movements and facial expressions such as nodding and smiling to show you understand.
3. Turn your body to face the person.
4. Let the speaker finish before you start to speak; do not interrupt.
5. Finish listening before thinking about what you are going to say next.
6. Ask open questions that give the other person a chance to say how they are feeling, e.g. 'How . . .?', 'What . . .?', 'Why . . .?'

An active listener

✔ Tick the correct answers.

1. When someone is speaking to me I should . . .
   a) look straight at them
   b) turn my body so my ear is facing them
   c) put my hand on them
   d) look at the ground

2. This is called . . .
   a) eye contact
   b) face contact
   c) ear contact
   d) hand contact

3. A good listener . . .
   a) does not interrupt
   b) pays close attention to the other person's words, body language and tone of voice
   c) waits for their turn to speak
   d) all of the above

4. Waiting for your turn to speak means . . .
   a) interrupting the speaker so that you can speak ☐
   b) waiting for the speaker to finish while thinking
      about what you're going to say next ☐
   c) listening attentively to what the person has to
      say and then speaking at the appropriate time ☐

5. If someone misunderstands what you have said you could say . . .
   a) 'If you'd listened you'd understand' ☐
   b) 'Nothing – it doesn't matter' ☐
   c) 'You obviously weren't listening' ☐
   d) 'What I meant to say was . . .' ☐

6. If you're unsure about what someone else has said to you, you could say . . .
   a) 'I think what you mean is . . .' ☐
   b) 'Whaaa?' ☐
   c) 'I can't understand you' ☐
   d) 'I haven't a clue what you're talking about' ☐

Learning *Keepsake*

Three things I have learned about how to listen are:

1. _____
2. _____
3. _____

As a result of what I have learned about listening, I will:
_____
_____
_____

_____ has shared this Learning Keepsake with me _____

Name of student   Parent's/guardian's signature

LESSON 13
Passive, Assertive and Aggressive Communication

At the end of this lesson . . .
. . . you will know about different types of communication
. . . and you will have learned some skills to help you solve disagreements.

Key Words
- Passive
- Aggressive
- Assertive
- Communication

 # Keyskill
- Communicating

Different types of communication

- **Passive** communication is when you do not stand up for yourself. You do not say how you really feel or what you want. You let others push you around. A passive person could be described as timid, a person pleaser, a doormat or a pushover.
- **Aggressive** communication is trying to get what you want by bullying or disrespecting others. An aggressive person could be described as pushy, a bully or overpowering.
- **Assertive** communication means truthfully and honestly saying how you feel while also respecting the other person. An assertive person could be described as confident, calm, honest, strong, or self-assured.

Sometimes a person will behave passively, sometimes aggressively and at other times they will be assertive. In most cases assertive communication is the best option.

Individual Activity

The pictures below demonstrate the three main styles of communication: passive, aggressive and assertive. The girl on the left has borrowed her friend's bicycle and returned it with a puncture. In each case, describe the behaviour and body language of the person who owns the bicycle and say which type of communication they are using.

Uh, ah, thanks.

Here is your bike back.

Thank you for returning it. Have you noticed that there is a puncture on the front wheel?

Here is your bike back.

Well that's the last time you'll get it, idiot. It's punctured!

Here is your bike back.

1. _____

_____

_____

_____

_____

_____

2. _____

_____

_____

_____

_____

_____

3. _____

_____

_____

_____

_____

_____

Class Activity

For each picture:

1. How do you think the person who owns the bicycle is feeling?
2. How do you think the person who borrowed the bicycle is feeling?
3. Which response do you consider most appropriate in this case? Why?
4. Why is it difficult to be assertive with some people and not with others?

Tips for assertive communication

1. Repeat your point quietly but firmly, paying attention to your body language and tone of voice. Stay calm but confident.
2. Be prepared to say No if someone is trying to pressure you into doing something you do not want to do.
3. Keep to your point and don't be drawn into disagreements that have nothing to do with the subject at issue.
4. Don't allow others make you feel guilty about being assertive.

Group Activity

In your group, discuss the questions below to help you decide whether or not it is always appropriate to use assertive behaviour.

1. Do you think assertive communication is always appropriate? Why/why not?
2. Describe a situation where a passive response might be appropriate.
3. Do you think that there are certain situations in which an aggressive response is unavoidable? Why/why not?
4. How does our relationship with a person affect our dealings with them?

Pair Activity

Read the following scenario taken from everyday experience and role play the situation using each of the communication styles (passive, aggressive, assertive). Does the outcome change depending on the type of communication used? Why/why not?

You are sitting at home watching your favourite television programme when your brother comes in, takes the remote control and switches channels.

Now pick other situations that young people encounter every day, role play these situations using the different types of communication e.g. the teacher blames you in the wrong for talking.

Learning *Keepsake*

Three things I have learned about communication styles are:

1. _____
2. _____
3. _____

As a result of what I have learned about effective communication, I will:

_____
_____
_____

_____ has shared this Learning Keepsake with me _____
Name of student   Parent's/guardian's signature

Topic Review

Date / /

In this topic I learned about
_____

This topic is useful to me in my life because
_____
_____

In this topic I liked
_____
_____

In this topic I did not like
_____
_____

I would like to find out more about
_____
_____

Key Skills I have used in this topic are:

- ☐ Managing myself
- ☐ Staying well
- ☐ Communicating
- ☐ Being creative
- ☐ Working with others
- ☐ Managing information and thinking

*Are you up for the challenge?

With your class, create and produce a drama that demonstrates the importance of effective communication.

TOPIC 5

Being Healthy

LESSON 14
Body Care

At the end of this lesson . . .

. . . you will know the importance of personal hygiene in adolescence

. . . and you will have explored the link between good personal hygiene and self-confidence.

Key Words
- Hygiene
- Perspiration

Keyskill
- Staying well

Individual Activity

Look at the different parts of the body labeled below. For each body part describe the personal hygiene steps that need to be taken and how often.

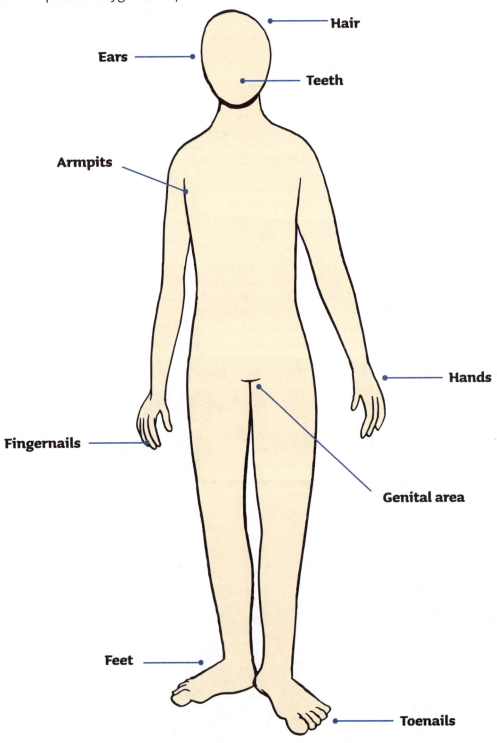

Hair

Ears

Teeth

Armpits

Hands

Fingernails

Genital area

Feet

Toenails

Group Activity

In your group, answer the following questions.

1. Why is it particularly important for teenagers to appreciate the need for personal hygiene?

   _____

   _____

   _____

2. How do teenagers learn about personal hygiene?

   _____

   _____

3. What might prevent a teenager from having good personal hygiene? How could this be solved?

   _____

   _____

4. What could/should you do if someone you knew had poor personal hygiene? What would you need to consider before deciding what to do?

   _____

   _____

Why is personal hygiene important?

Under the headings below, list the reasons why it is important to have good personal hygiene.

Physical – your body 	Emotional – how you feel 	Social – relationships 

Good personal hygiene is important for our physical, emotional and social wellbeing. The following areas require attention in order to maintain good personal hygiene.

Body

It is important for teenagers to shower every day to prevent body odour. Sweat, which regulates the body's temperature, is formed when the body gets too warm. Body odour (BO) is caused when sweat comes into contact with germs on the skin. Regular showering, combined with using a deodorant or antiperspirant, can help to prevent BO. Roll-on deodorants and antiperspirants are kinder to the environment than sprays. Antiperspirants are more effective than deodorants for dealing with BO. Whichever is chosen, it must be used in addition to showering.

Clothes

Underwear and socks should be changed every day to reduce the build-up of germs that can lead to BO. It is also important to wear clean clothes that have been dried properly.

Skin

It is natural for teenagers to get spots. During puberty the oil glands in skin become more active, so skin care is particularly important at this age. Acne is a skin condition that occurs during puberty: it takes different forms and can be minor or more severe. It is not caused by poor hygiene, but it is important to take good care of your skin if you have acne. Medicated pads, which can be bought from a pharmacy, can help with spots. In some cases it may be necessary to seek the advice of your doctor in dealing with acne.

Hair

Hair should be washed at least once a week. If the hair is greasy it might have to be washed more often. Always comb hair thoroughly and check your hair regularly for head lice. An itchy scalp can be a sign of dandruff or head lice. A pharmacist will give advice on suitable treatments.

Teeth

Make sure you brush your teeth in the morning and at night. It is important to change your toothbrush every three months and to make regular visits to the dentist.

Hands

It is important to wash your hands regularly to prevent germs spreading. You should always wash your hands after using the toilet and before and after handling food.

Hygiene crossword

Across

4 An itchy scalp may mean you have this condition.

5 A skin condition that occurs at puberty.

6 Regulates the body temperature.

7 You should change your toothbrush every ———— months.

Down

1 This is more effective than a deodorant at preventing odour.

2 These pads can help prevent spots.

3 Spots occur when these become blocked with dirt and grease.

4 Consult this person if acne is severe.

Learning *Keepsake*

Three things I have learned about body care are:

1. _____
2. _____
3. _____

As a result of what I have learned about maintaining personal hygiene, I will:

_____
_____
_____

_____ has shared this Learning Keepsake with me _____

Name of student   Parent's/guardian's signature

LESSON 15
Healthy Eating

At the end of this lesson . . .
. . . you will understand what a balanced diet is
. . . and appreciate the relationship between a
balanced diet and good health.

Key Words
- Food pyramid
- Portions

Keyskill
- Staying well

Individual Activity

In the table below, write down everything you ate and drank yesterday.

Breakfast	
Lunch	
Dinner	
Snacks	
Drinks	

A balanced diet

A balanced diet contains the recommended amounts of carbohydrates (including fibre), fats, proteins, vitamins, minerals and water.

The food pyramid is a good guide to a balanced diet.

What is a portion?

Fats, oils, sweets, cakes, fizzy drinks, crisps: should be used/eaten sparingly

Meat, fish and alternatives: 2 servings per day.
1 breast chicken · 1 fillet fish · 2 eggs · 1 pork/lamb chop · 6 tablespoons peas/beans/lentils · 2 ounces meat

Milk, cheese and yoghurt: 5 servings per day.
1 glass milk · 1 small carton yoghurt · 1 small yoghurt drink · 1 matchbox-sized portion hard cheese · 1 slice pizza/lasagne/quiche · 1 mug hot chocolate made with milk · 1 smoothie

Fruit and vegetables: 5 servings per day.
1 piece of fruit · ½ glass fruit juice 2 tablespoons · cooked vegetables 1 helping salad · 3 spoons tinned fruit

Breads, cereals and potatoes:
6 servings per day. 1 small bowl breakfast cereal · 1 slice bread · 1 small roll · 1 pitta · ½ bagel or ciabatta · 1 small potato · 2 crackers/rice cakes · 1 handful (uncooked) rice/pasta/noodles

Look back at what you ate yesterday and fill in or draw what you ate on the correct food shelf. For example, if you ate yoghurt, write or draw a carton of yogurt on the 'Milk, cheese and yoghurt' shelf. Remember to include any snacks you had. For each shelf add up your servings. Compare these results to the recommended servings on p88.

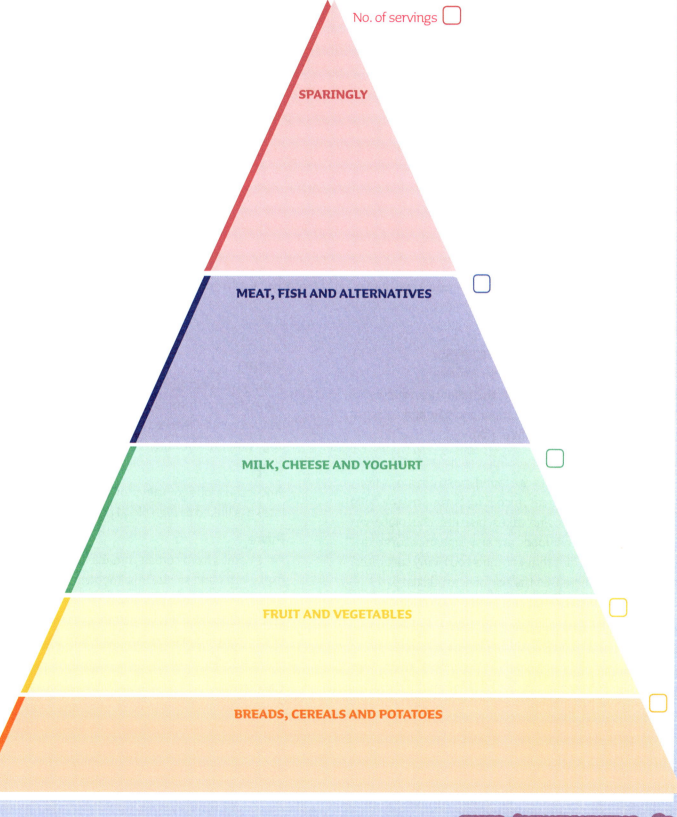

No. of servings ☐

SPARINGLY

MEAT, FISH AND ALTERNATIVES ☐

MILK, CHEESE AND YOGHURT ☐

FRUIT AND VEGETABLES ☐

BREADS, CEREALS AND POTATOES ☐

1. What does your pyramid tell you about your diet?

2. Are there any food groups that you are eating too much from?

3. Are there any food groups that you are eating too little from?

4. Why is it important not to eat too many foods from the top shelf?

Good food choices

Teenagers can make their diet healthier by choosing less fat, sugar and salt and eating an adequate amount of fibre.

Fats

Saturated fats are found mostly in foods from animal sources, including butter, cream, solid frying fats; and cakes, biscuits, chocolate and crisps. Fast foods are also high in saturated fats. A diet that contains too many saturated fats increases the risk of heart disease.

Unsaturated fats are found in olive oil, peanuts and soya beans; these can have a positive benefit by lowering cholesterol. Cholesterol is a type of fat found in all animal cells. It has important functions in the body, but too much cholesterol is unhealthy and can result from eating too many saturated fats.

Sugar

Sugar gives energy, but it has little nutritional value. Too much sugar can cause obesity and dental disease. Sweets and fizzy drinks contain large amounts of sugar.

Salt

Processed foods contain s lot of salt. A high salt intake is linked to high blood pressure.

Fibre

Fibre comes from cereals, breads, vegetables, fruits, nuts and seeds. It is important for good digestion and it can help lower cholesterol and control blood sugar levels. Wholegrain and wholemeal breads contain more fibre than white bread.

Calcium

Calcium is needed to build strong bones and help prevent osteoporosis in later life. Calcium is also important for healthy teeth. Milk, cheese and yoghurt are rich sources of calcium.

What to eat and why

A healthy diet is important during adolescence as this is a time when the body is developing and growing quickly. Eating the right types of food can:

- give you more energy
- help develop healthy skin, hair, nails and teeth
- develop stronger muscles
- help you concentrate in school and study for exams
- help you feel more healthy.

Around the plates on the next page, create three healthy meals for yourself. Make sure to include a balance of foods from the food pyramid in your selection. Choose two healthy snacks that could be eaten between meals.

Healthy Mealtimes

Breakfast

Lunch

Dinner

Learning *Keepsake*

Three things I have learned about healthy eating are:

1. _____
2. _____
3. _____

As a result of what I have learned about eating healthily, I will:
_____
_____
_____

_____ has shared this Learning Keepsake with me _____

Name of student   Parent's/guardian's signature

LESSON 16
Exercise

At the end of this lesson . . .
. . . you will know about the importance of physical exercise, rest and sleep
. . . and have drawn up a personal exercise plan.

Key Words
- Exercise
- Pulse

 # Keyskill
- Staying well

As well as a healthy diet, regular exercise, adequate rest and sleep are very important for teenagers. Teenagers need nine or more hours of sleep a night. A continued lack of sleep can affect how the brain functions: many teenagers notice a relationship between the amount of sleep they get and how they feel the next day. A healthy heart helps a person to live their lives fully and with enjoyment – this is why exercise is so important.

Measuring your heart rate

Checking your pulse rate at rest, during exercise and immediately after vigorous exercise can give you important information about your overall fitness level.

How can you check your pulse?

You can find your pulse in a few places on your body. The easiest place to check your pulse is on your wrist or your neck.

To measure the pulse on your wrist:
- Hold your hand in front of you.
- Gently place two fingers of your other hand (any two except your thumb – because your thumb has its own pulse) at the top of your wrist.
- Move your fingers until you feel a steady beat.
- Count the number of beats for 15 seconds, then multiply that number by 4 to get your pulse rate per minute. For example, if you counted 20 beats during the 15 seconds your pulse is 80bpm (beats per minute).

To measure the pulse on your neck:
- Gently place two fingers (not your thumb) just below your jaw and to either side of your windpipe.
- Move your fingers until you feel a steady beat.
- Count the beats for 15 seconds, then multiply that number by 4 to get your pulse rate per minute.

Individual Activity

Your resting heart rate is the number of beats per minute when the body is at rest.

1. Follow the instructions above to find your resting heart rate and write it down.
   _____

2. Now stand up. On your teacher's command, run on the spot for two minutes.

3. Sit down and rest, recording your heart rate every minute until it returns to your resting heart rate.

- Heart rate after 1 minute: _____
- Heart rate after 2 minutes: _____
- Heart rate after 3 minutes: _____
- Heart rate after 4 minutes: _____

Class Activity

Now answer the following questions.

1. At the beginning of the exercise, what was the average resting heart rate of all the students? (Find this figure by adding up everyone's resting heart rate and dividing this number by the total number of students.)

2. What is the average heart rate immediately after exercise?

3. How does jogging on the spot affect the heart rate? Why do you think this happens?

   _____
   _____
   _____

4. What was the fastest recovery time and what was the slowest recovery time in the class?

   Fastest recovery time   Slowest recovery time

What it all means

The amount of time the heart takes to return to a normal at-rest rate after exercise is called recovery time. This is a measure of our body's general fitness. The shorter the recovery time, the higher the level of fitness.

Average heart rates for various age groups

AGE	PULSE RATE (BPM)
Babies under 1 year	100–160
Children aged 1–10	60–140
Children aged 10+ and adults	60–100
Well-conditionead athletes	40–60

At rest, your heart beats at a slower rate and there is little demand put on it. During exercise, the heart has to beat faster to supply the muscles with oxygen.

Like any muscle, the heart needs to be exercised to become stronger. Any exercise that raises your heart rate and makes you feel warm helps to strengthen your heart. To keep physically fit you need to do 60 minutes of moderate to vigorous activity at least five times a week.

Different types of exercise

Moderate exercise

Heart beats faster than normal
Breathing is harder than normal

- Walking
- Cycling
- Roller skating

Vigorous exercise

Heart beats a lot faster than normal
Breathing is a lot harder than normal

- Hurling/rugby/soccer
- Tennis
- Running
- Martial arts

Can you add any other activities?

_____

_____

Individual Activity

Your task for the next few weeks is to organise an exercise programme. Remember to factor in some good nights of sleep too. Use the prompts below to help you create an exercise plan.

Keep a record of your progress in the table provided on the next page.

I plan to be active for _____ this week.

I will participate in the following activities:

_____

_____

_____

_____

_____

My goals in exercising are:

1. _____

2. _____

3. _____

If you are not normally physically active:

1. Start slowly. Build up to an extra 15–30 minutes of moderate-intensity activity 1–2 days a week.

2. Once you reach this level, aim for 30 minutes of activity on most days of the week. For example, progress from 30 minutes on 2–3 days a week to 30 minutes on 3–4 days a week.

3. As you progress, you will get closer to the goal of 60 minutes or more of moderate to vigorous activity every day.

Source: *Get Ireland Active* (promoting physical activity in Ireland), National Guidelines on Physical Activity in Ireland. Go to www.getactiveireland.ie for more information

	Type of exercise	Duration of exercise	Did you achieve your goal?	Did you get 9 hours' sleep that night?
Monday				
Tuesday				
Wednesday				
Thursday				
Friday				
Saturday				
Sunday				

You can spread the amount of exercise you get in one day over the whole day.
For example:

Cycling to school	10 minutes
Playing soccer at break	15 minutes
Having a kick-about with your sister	10 minutes
Walking to the shop	5 minutes
Hoovering your bedroom	10 minutes

Learning Keepsake

Three things I have learned about exercise and rest are:

1. _____
2. _____
3. _____

As a result of what I have learned about exercise and rest, I will:

_____
_____
_____

_____ has shared this Learning Keepsake with me _____

Name of student   Parent's/guardian's signature

LESSON 17

Looking after Myself

At the end of this lesson . . .

. . . you will have examined ways of keeping safe . . . and be aware of the best response in risky situations.

Key Words
- Risk

 # Keyskill
- Managing myself

Risky Business

Every day we are faced with risky situations, and sometimes bad things do happen to good people. It is important to be aware of possible risks to our safety.

Don't take unnecessary chances with your own safety. If you take risks with your safety you may also endanger others. You might think 'This will never happen to me,' but you can never be too careful.

A Typical Day in Tommy's Life

Look at a typical day in Tommy's life and using the pictures as prompts, identify some of the possible risks that he faces every day.

On the farm   Travelling to school

1. _____

2. _____

In school   At sports/physical activities

3. _____

4. _____

Online   Out and about

5. _____

6. _____

Do you think the risks that Tommy faces are typical for a young teenager in Ireland? Give reasons for your answer.

Can you think of other risky situations someone your age may find themselves in?

Identify which situation you think is most dangerous and explain why.

Stay safe!

On the farm
- Take extra care around farm machinery, slurry pits and water around the farm.
- Always show respect to animals and livestock on farms.

Travelling to school
- Always wear a helmet when cycling.

In school
- Be aware of risks and dangers in different rooms in school and on the corridors.

At activities
- Always follow pool rules and lifeguards' instructions.

Online
- Never give your personal details to anyone online.
- Always report cyber-bullying to a trusted adult.
- Don't give out your mobile phone number to strangers.

When travelling
- Always wait for a bus or a train that is well lit.
- Always sit up the front near other passengers when using public transport.
- Always tell somebody when you are leaving and what time you will be home.
- Always have extra money with you in case of emergency.
- Trust your instincts – if a situation feels unsafe, get out of there.

 ## Individual Activity

1. Identify a situation in the past when you felt you put your safety at risk.

2. Write down what you would do differently if you were in the same situation again.

Learning **Keepsake**

Three things I have learned about staying safe are:

1. _____

2. _____

3. _____

As a result of what I have learned about staying safe, I will:

_____

_____

_____

_____ has shared this Learning Keepsake with me _____

Name of student   Parent's/guardian's signature

LESSON 18

Fire Safety

At the end of this lesson . . .
. . . you will know the evacuation procedure in your home and at school.

Key Words
- Evacuation
- Fire drill

 # Keyskill
- Staying safe

Fires in the home are a major cause of deaths every year. But most house fires can be avoided and there is usually a simple method of prevention. It's hard to believe that something as simple as a phone charger, for example, could cause a fire. It is always important to have a fire evacuation procedure at home and at school.

 Weblink

Have a look at the cartoon from the National Fire Protection Association titled 'Exit Strategy' search for it on: www.youtube.com

Below is a list of some of the common causes of fires in the home. How could you ensure they are not a fire hazard? The first one has been done for you.

Cause of fire	Prevention
Open fires	Use a suitable fireguard

Christmas lights

Sockets, plugs and wires

Cigarettes

Nightwear

Candles

Matches

Chip pans

Chimneys

Phone chargers

Fire drill

When a fire breaks out things can happen very quickly, so it is important that your family has a rehearsed escape drill. A smoke alarm should be fitted at each level of the house and this smoke alarm should be checked once a week.

 Individual Activity

Below is an example of an escape route. Draw a similar map of your own house and design the escape route.

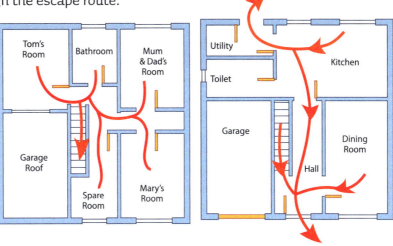

Points to consider:

- Make sure that there are two escape routes.
- Decide on a meeting point.
- It is important to keep all stairways clear.
- Practise the plan until perfect.
- If you're caught in a smoke-filled room, get down on your hands and knees. Smoke is hot, so it rises; this means that there is cleaner air to breathe below the smoke level.
- Get out as fast as you can.
- Close all doors behind you as you leave.
- Call the fire brigade, but don't call 999 until you are outside the house.
- If your clothes are on fire, stop, drop and roll. Do not run, as this makes the fire burn faster. Drop to the ground and roll until the fire is out.
- Never go back into the building.

 Class Activity

Imagine the fire alarm in your school has just sounded. Act out the evacuation procedures from the classroom where you are now to your evacuation point.

Learning *Keepsake*

Three things I have learned about fire safety are:

1. _____
2. _____
3. _____

As a result of what I have learned about fire safety, I will:

_____
_____
_____

_____ has shared this Learning Keepsake with me _____
Name of student   Parent's/guardian's signature

Topic Review

Date / /

In this topic I learned about

This topic is useful to me in my life because

In this topic I liked

In this topic I did not like

I would like to find out more about

Key Skills I have used in this topic are:

- ☐ Managing myself
- ☐ Staying well
- ☐ Communicating
- ☐ Being creative
- ☐ Working with others
- ☐ Managing information and thinking

*Are you up for the challenge?

Using what you have learned in this topic, carry out a survey to determine how healthy your class is. Present your findings to your class using PowerPoint, graphs, tables, etc.

TOPIC 6

Having a Friend, Being a Friend

- Lesson 19 Making New Friends

LESSON 19
Making New Friends

At the end of this lesson . . .
. . . you will know how to make friends
. . . and you will have explored the characteristics
of a good friend.

Key Words
- Friendship

Keyskill
- Working with others

Individual Activity

What characteristics are important in a good friend?
Write your ideas beside the photograph below.

Individual Activity

1. Which characteristics were the most important for friendship?
   _____
   _____

2. Do all your friends have all the characteristics that you admire or like in a friend?
   _____

3. When you were younger, how did you meet your friends?
   _____
   _____
   _____

4. Where can someone your age go to make new friends?
   _____
   _____

5. How important do you think the friends you make on social networking sites are to you?
   _____

6. How can you show your friends that you are a 'good friend' to them?
   _____
   _____

7. Are there times when a friendship cannot be saved? If so, how can you ensure you end the friendship respectfully?
   _____
   _____

A good friend . . .

1. Does not mind you having other friends.
2. Understands that you have to respect your parents.
3. Will keep your secrets.
4. Makes you feel good about yourself.
5. Doesn't try to put you down when you make a mistake or have a big success.
6. Does not say bad things about you behind your back.
7. Has your best interests at heart.
8. Is kind but truthful when you ask their advice or opinion.

Individual Activity

Using what you have learned about friendship, create a poster entitled 'Wanted: Good Friend'.

Learning *Keepsake*

Three things I have learned about making friends are:

1. _____
2. _____
3. _____

As a result of what I have learned about friendship, I will:

_____

_____

_____

_____ has shared this Learning Keepsake with me _____

Name of student   Parent's/guardian's signature

Topic Review

Date / /

In this topic I learned about
_____

This topic is useful to me in my life because
_____
_____

In this topic I liked
_____
_____

In this topic I did not like
_____
_____

I would like to find out more about
_____
_____

Key Skills I have used in this topic are:

- ☐ Managing myself
- ☐ Staying well
- ☐ Communicating
- ☐ Being creative
- ☐ Working with others
- ☐ Managing information and thinking

*Are you up for the challenge?

Make a friendship tree for display in your class. Each student sticks a leaf to the tree. Each leaf contains the statement. 'A friend to me is someone who ...'

Positive Mental Health

LESSON 20

Me as Unique and Different

At the end of this lesson . . .
. . . you will recognise your own talents and those of others.

Key Words
- Assertive
- Self-esteem
- Confidence

Keyskill
- Working with others

What is self-esteem?

Self-esteem means valuing and respecting yourself as a person. It means recognising your strengths, having respect for yourself, and being able to stand up for yourself in an assertive way.

To have healthy self-esteem, it is essential to recognise what you are good at. This is different from being boastful – it means that you know your own strengths. This gives you confidence, thus building your self-esteem.

Individual Activity

Using the letters of your first name, make a list of the positive things about yourself on a large poster sheet. Here is Tim's example.

Thoughtful towards others
Imaginative
Marvellous at Rugby

Pair Activity

Now use the letters in the name of the person beside you to make a list of positive things about them.

Was it easy or difficult to come up with your own strengths? Give reasons for your answer.

_____

_____

Was it easy or difficult to come up with your partner's strengths? Why do you think this is?

_____

_____

_____

_____

What people or things help us to recognise our own strengths?

_____

_____

_____

 ## Group Activity

In groups, discuss the things that can improve self-esteem and the things that can damage self-esteem.

Self-esteem bashers	Self-esteem boosters
Things that make people feel bad about themselves	Things that make people feel good about themselves

 ## Individual Activity

Using what you have learned about your own talents and strengths, fill in your curriculum vitae. A curriculum vitae or CV is a form that a person fills out when they are applying for a job. It gives them the opportunity to tell the employer their own particular strengths and talents.

Curriculum Vitae

Name:

_____

Address

Education to date

Primary:

_____
_____

Secondary:

_____
_____

Interests:

_____
_____

Hobbies:

_____
_____

Achievements to date:

_____
_____

Challenges to date:

_____
_____

Ambitions:

_____
_____

Something I am proud of:

_____
_____

Any other information you would like to add:

_____
_____

Learning *Keepsake*

Three things I have learned about self-esteem are:

1. _____
2. _____
3. _____

As a result of what I have learned about self-esteem, I will:

_____
_____
_____

_____ has shared this Learning Keepsake with me _____
Name of student   Parent's/guardian's signature

LESSON 21

My Heroes

At the end of this lesson . . .

. . . you will be more aware of the people who influence you

. . . you will have examined how and why people influence you

. . . and you will respect each person's individuality.

Key Words
- Influences
- Decisions

Keyskill
- Being creative

Heroes

Have you ever asked yourself the question, 'Who influences me?' Probably not, because a lot of the time we are unaware of other people's influences on us.

Each day people influence the decisions we make. The latest fashions may influence what you wear; a family member or teacher may influence the career path you take; an advertisement may persuade you to buy a particular product.

Individual Activity

Using the pictures as prompts. and list the different ways these people can influence someone your age.

Sports person

Parents

Friends

Celebrity

Teachers

Politicians

Now try to identify the people who influence you. Write the most influential people in your life in the circle.

Circle of Influence

Write down 3 ways you influence others positively and negatively.

Positive

1. _____
2. _____
3. _____

Negative

1. _____
2. _____
3. _____

Group Activity

Read the lyrics or listen to the song *Wind Beneath My Wings* and brainstorm what you think makes a person a hero.

Wind Beneath my Wings

Oh, oh, oh, oh, oh.
It must have been cold there in my shadow,
to never have sunlight on your face.
You were content to let me shine, that's your way.
You always walked a step behind.

So I was the one with all the glory,
while you were the one with all the strength.
A beautiful face without a name for so long.
A beautiful smile to hide the pain.

Did you ever know that you're my hero,
and everything I would like to be?
I can fly higher than an eagle,
'cause you are the wind beneath my wings.

It might have appeared to go unnoticed,
but I've got it all here in my heart.
I want you to know I know the truth, of course I know it.
I would be nothing without you.

Did you ever know that you're my hero?
You're everything I wish I could be.
I could fly higher than an eagle,
'cause you are the wind beneath my wings.

Did I ever tell you you're my hero?
You're everything, everything I wish I could be.
Oh, and I, I could fly higher than an eagle,
'cause you are the wind beneath my wings,
'cause you are the wind beneath my wings.

Oh, the wind beneath my wings.
You, you, you, you are the wind beneath my wings.
Fly, fly, fly away. You let me fly so high.
Oh, you, you, you, the wind beneath my wings.
Oh, you, you, you, the wind beneath my wings.

Fly, fly, fly high against the sky,
so high I almost touch the sky.
Thank you, thank you,
thank God for you, the wind beneath my wings.

Create a profile of your hero below. Add a picture of your hero in the space provided.

My Hero

Name: _____

About my hero:

Nationality

_____

Qualities

_____

_____

_____

Reasons I admire my hero

_____

_____

_____

_____

My message to my hero

_____

_____

_____

_____

_____

_____

_____

_____

_____

_____

_____

Learning *Keepsake*

Three things I have learned about the influences in my life are:

1. _____
2. _____
3. _____

As a result of what I have learned about these influences, I will:

_____
_____
_____

_____ has shared this Learning Keepsake with me _____

Name of student   Parent's/guardian's signature

LESSON 22

Special Relationships

At the end of this lesson . . .

. . . you will appreciate your responsibilities in different relationships.

Key Words
- Relationships
- Responsibilities
- Characteristics

 # Keyskill
- Communicating

Relationships are a two-way process. In every relationship there is give and take. The things that we get from a relationship include love, support, advice, etc. We must also recognise that we have a responsibility to do things for other people.

Pair Activity

Write down two responsibilities that each of the people in the following relationships have to each other.

Boyfriend to girlfriend

1. _____

2. _____

Girlfriend to boyfriend

1. _____

2. _____

Parents to teenage child

1. _____

2. _____

Teenage child to parent

1. _____

2. _____

Coach to player

1. _____

2. _____

Player to coach

1. _____

2. _____

Teacher to student

1. _____

2. _____

Student to teacher

1. _____

2. _____

Grandparent to teenage grandson/granddaughter

1. _____

2. _____

Teenage grandson/granddaughter to grandparent

1. _____

2. _____

Class Activity

1. Which of the relationships could you identify with?
2. Are there any similarities between the responsibilities that everyone has? Explain your answer.
3. Do you think that your responsibilities change as you get older? Give reasons for your answer.
4. Identify and discuss some of the problems that can arise in the following relationships if people do not carry out their responsibilities. How can these problems be resolved?

Relationship	Problem	How it could be resolved
Boyfriend/girlfriend		
Coach/player		
Teacher/student		
Parent/child		

My relationships

Think about a relationship that you have had since childhood. Write down who the relationship is with and write down two responsibilities you have to this person.

Relationship	How my responsibilities have changed
Three things that make this relationship successful	
Three things that would cause conflict between us	

Learning *Keepsake*

Three things I have learned about relationships are:

1. _____
2. _____
3. _____

As a result of what I have learned about relationships, I will:

_____
_____
_____

_____ has shared this Learning Keepsake with me _____

Name of student   Parent's/guardian's signature

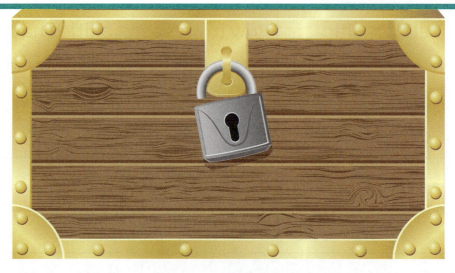

Topic Review

Date / /

In this topic I learned about
_____

This topic is useful to me in my life because
_____
_____

In this topic I liked
_____
_____

In this topic I did not like
_____
_____

I would like to find out more about
_____
_____

Key Skills I have used in this topic are:

- ☐ Managing myself
- ☐ Staying well
- ☐ Communicating
- ☐ Being creative
- ☐ Working with others
- ☐ Managing information and thinking

*Are you up for the challenge?

Complete a project on your hero, include pictures, biographical details and an interview if possible.

TOPIC 8

Being an Adolescent

LESSON 23

Changes at Adolescence

At the end of this lesson . . .

. . . you will understand the changes that occur during adolescence.

Key Words
- Puberty
- Adolescence

 # Keyskill
- Managing myself

The best thing about being a teenager is …

_____

The worst thing about being a teenager is …

_____

Puberty

During puberty the hormone levels in our bodies change and this in turn causes the body to change in various ways. People's feelings and emotions also change as they are grow from childhood to adulthood. Because everyone is unique, puberty begins at different times for each person. For most people puberty begins between the ages of 10 and 16, although it can start earlier or later.

Identify the changes that occur during puberty for females

Identify the changes that occur during puberty for males

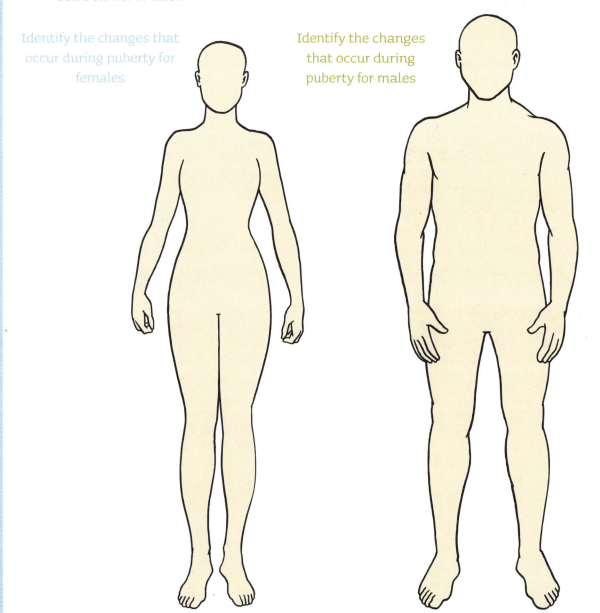

Changes

As well as experiencing physical changes during puberty, you also experience social and emotional changes.

Emotional changes relate to changes in our moods and feelings, these occur because our brains are teaching us how to express our feelings in a grown up way.

Social changes relate to changes in the way we interact with others and changes in the way we see ourselves. We are seeking more independence and examining where we fit in.

Class Activity

As a class look back at your answers to the first activity on the best and worst thing about being a teenager and suggest whether they come under physical, social or emotional changes. Fill in what your class comes up with in the table below.

Social	Emotional	Physical

Individual Activity

Write a paragraph outlining any changes that have occurred in your appearance, your thoughts and feelings and your friendships in the last year.

Learning *Keepsake*

Three things I have learned about changes in adolescence are:

1. _____
2. _____
3. _____

As a result of what I have learned about puberty, I will:

_____

_____

_____

_____ has shared this Learning Keepsake with me _____

Name of student   Parent's/guardian's signature

LESSON 24

Recognising Feelings

At the end of this lesson . . .

. . . you will have increased your awareness of common emotions and words to express them . . . and you will be aware of appropriate ways of expressing your emotions.

Key Words
- Appropriate
- Inappropriate
- Emotions
- Feelings

Keyskill
- Communicating

Class Activity

Below are examples of common feelings. Add any you can think of that have not been included.

Aggressive   Anxious   Apologetic   Arrogant   Bashful   Happy   Horrified   Hurt

Blissful   Bored   Cautious   Determined   Confident   Hysterical   Indifferent   Interested

Pick one feeling and say what happened to make you feel this way

_____

_____

Class Activity

Feelings are neither good nor bad. However, it is important to deal with feelings in an appropriate way. Inappropriate responses to feelings can damage relationships. Read the following story and consider the responses.

Feeling Hurt

Jean is a first-year student. Since she started secondary school she has been very friendly with Ruth. One day, just before basketball training, Jean overhears Ruth talking about her behind her back with two other students, Sarah and Lorna.

Inappropriate responses:
- Jean rushes up to Ruth and shouts at her.
- Jean ignores Ruth for two months.
- Jean pretends she didn't hear anything but promises herself she will get back at Ruth.

 ## Class Activity

Why are the previous responses not appropriate?

Appropriate responses:
- Jean admits to Ruth that she overheard her and that she is hurt.
- Jean decides to forget about it because Ruth has been a good friend up to now.
- Jean makes a joke of it with Ruth, letting Ruth know that she has heard the conversation but that she forgives her.

Why are these responses appropriate?

 ## Individual Activity

Read the following stories and write down appropriate and inappropriate responses to the situations.

You are training with the school football team. The coach has made it very clear that commitment is really valued, and he told the team at the start of the season that he will only play people who attend training. One of the other players, who is very talented, has missed a lot of training sessions. Just before the first championship game you learn that you have been dropped and the other player has been picked ahead of you.

How would you feel in this scenario?_____
Inappropriate ways of responding:
_____
_____
_____

Give reasons for your answer.
_____
_____
_____

Appropriate ways of responding:
_____
_____
_____

Give reasons for your answer.

_____

_____

_____

Teacher's Pet

Your teacher has set your group a project to complete for SPHE class. One of the other group members is very bossy and keeps forcing her opinions on your group. You really want to have some input but you are finding it difficult to get through.

How would you feel in this scenario? _____

Inappropriate ways of expressing how you feel:

_____

_____

_____

Give reasons for your answer.

_____

_____

_____

Appropriate ways of expressing how you feel:

_____

_____

_____

Give reasons for your answer.

_____

_____

_____

 Group Activity Class Activity

Compare your answers with other people in your group.

Appropriate vs. inappropriate responses

In Jean's story above, the characters had very strong feelings. Feelings are never right or wrong – they just are. But people can control how they express their feelings. It is important to respect other people's feelings when expressing your own.

Write down a time when you expressed your feelings in an inappropriate way.

Suggest a more appropriate way you could have expressed how you felt.

Learning *Keepsake*

Three things I have learned about expressing feelings are:

1. _____
2. _____
3. _____

As a result of what I have learned about expressing my feelings, I will:

_____

_____

_____

_____ has shared this Learning Keepsake with me _____

Name of student   Parent's/guardian's signature

LESSON 25

Respecting my Feelings and the Feelings of Others

At the end of this lesson . . .
. . . you will be more aware of other peoples' feelings.

Key Words
- Facial expression
- Gestures
- Posture

 # Keyskill
- Working with others

Recognising how others are feeling

Look at the pictures below write down how you think the person in each picture is feeling and explain why do you think this. Make reference to posture, gestures and facial expressions.

How is the person feeling?_____
Why do you think this? _____
_____

How is the person feeling?_____
Why do you think this? _____
_____

How is the person feeling?_____
Why do you think this? _____
_____

How is the person feeling?_____
Why do you think this? _____
_____

How is the person feeling?_____
Why do you think this? _____
_____

How is the person feeling?_____
Why do you think this? _____
_____

How is the person feeling?_____
Why do you think this? _____
_____

Class Activity

For each picture suggest how you could show respect for the other person's feelings.

_____
_____
_____
_____
_____
_____
_____

Individual Activity

1. Why is it important to be able to recognise other people's feelings?
    _____
    _____

2. List three emotions that are considered acceptable.
    a) _____
    b) _____
    c) _____

3. List three emotions that are considered unacceptable.
    a) _____
    b) _____
    c) _____

4. Why do you think some emotions are more acceptable than others?
    _____
    _____
    _____
    _____

5. Do boys and girls express their emotions differently?
    _____
    _____

Class Activity

Choose one emotion and take turns at acting it out non-verbally. The rest of the class must guess the emotion.

Pay attention to:

Gestures
Facial expressions
Posture

Learning **Keepsake**

Three things I have learned about respecting other people's feelings are:

1. _____
2. _____
3. _____

As a result of what I have learned about respecting people's feelings, I will:
_____
_____
_____

_____ has shared this Learning Keepsake with me _____

Name of student   Parent's/guardian's signature

Topic Review

Date   /   /

In this topic I learned about
_____

This topic is useful to me in my life because
_____
_____

In this topic I liked
_____
_____

In this topic I did not like
_____
_____

I would like to find out more about
_____
_____

Key Skills I have used in this topic are:

☐ Managing myself
☐ Staying well
☐ Communicating
☐ Being creative
☐ Working with others
☐ Managing information and thinking

*Are you up for the challenge?
Write a daily diary recording your feelings and emotions for a week.

TOPIC 9

Sexuality and Sexual Health

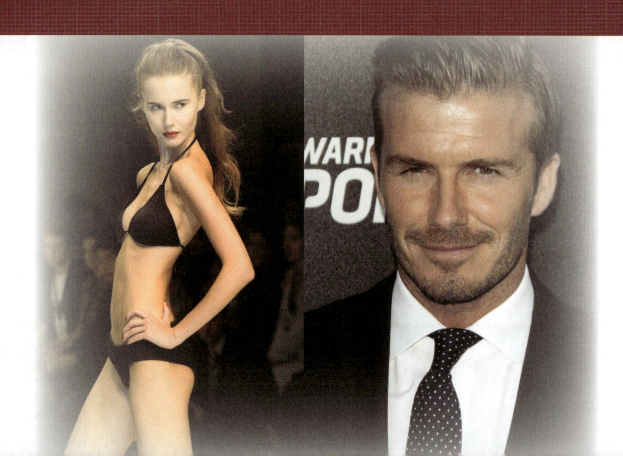

LESSON 26

The Reproductive System

At the end of this lesson . . .

. . . you will have a clear understanding of the male and female reproductive systems.

Key Words
- Reproductive system

Keyskill
- Managing myself

You will have learned about the male and female reproductive systems in SPHE class in primary school. Now let's look at how much you remember. Use the words in the list below to label the diagrams.

Fallopian tubes   penis   ovaries   bladder   vas deferens   scrotum
vulva   vagina   urethra   cervix   prostate gland   semen   uterus

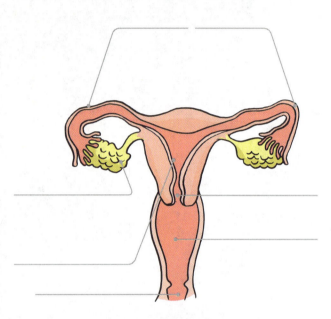
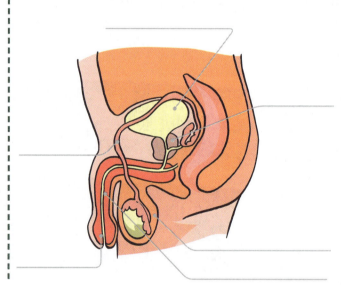

Class Activity

Discuss your answers with your teacher and make a note of the correct answers. Check your knowledge of the male and female reproductive systems by matching the following descriptions with the words from the previous task.

1. Two small organs that produce eggs _____

2. Two narrow tubes that join the ovaries to the uterus, through which the eggs pass

_____

3. The _____ holds the baby during pregnancy: it is also called the womb.

4. The neck of the womb, which connects the vagina to the uterus. During childbirth this canal gets much wider to let the baby through _____

5. The tube that connects the uterus to the outside of the body: the baby passes through this during birth _____

6. Where sperm are produced _____

7. These tubes carry the sperm _____

8. Produces a protective fluid for the sperm _____

9. This fluid carries sperm _____

10. A sac-like pouch that holds the testes; it hangs outside the body, which enables the sperm to survive _____

11. Sperm leaves the body through this tube _____

12. Sperm is carried from the testes to the urethra through these _____

13. The male external reproductive organ; it has an opening at the top that carries urine and semen from the body _____

Reproduction crossword

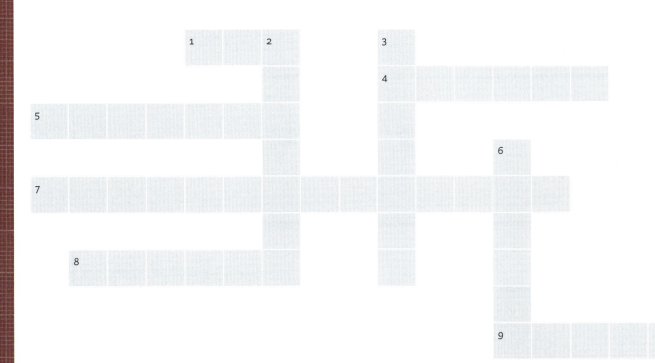

Across
1 The number of ovaries a woman has
4 The neck of the womb
5 Sperm leaves the penis through this tube
7 These connect the uterus to the ovaries
8 The baby lives here during pregnancy
9 Sperm is carried in this fluid

Down
2 These produce eggs
3 This pouch holds the testes
6 These produce sperm

Learning *Keepsake*

Three things I have learned about the reproductive system are:

1. _____
2. _____
3. _____

As a result of what I have learned about reproduction, I will:

_____
_____
_____

_____ has shared this Learning Keepsake with me _____

Name of student   Parent's/guardian's signature

LESSON 27

Sexual Intercourse and Conception

At the end of this lesson . . .
. . . you will understand how conception occurs

Key Words
- Intercourse
- Conception
- Menstruation

 # Keyskill
- Managing myself

Check your knowledge

Each stage of the menstrual cycle has been mixed up below. Put the stages in the correct order by labelling the explanations A, B, C, D.

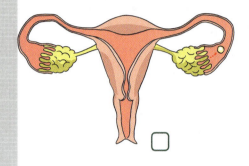

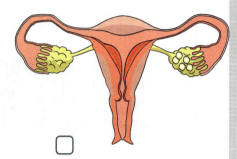

□

□

A. After a girl's period the lining of the uterus builds up with blood and tissue in preparation for a fertilised egg. □

B. The egg travels down the fallopian tube. □

C. About mid-cycle, hormones signal an ovary to release an egg. □

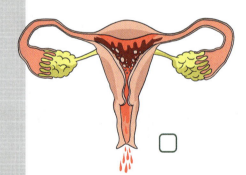

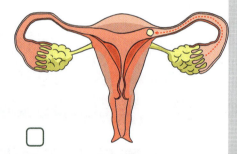

□

□

D. When the egg is not fertilised the lining of the uterus is no longer needed hormones signal the lining to breakdown and blood and tissue leave the body through the vagina. This is called the girl's period. □

Irregular Periods

It is quite normal for a teenage girl's periods to be irregular. Also, if a girl is feeling upset or worried or there is a change in their usual routine, a girls periods can be delayed or even stop.

Class Activity

Discuss the stages in menstruation with your teacher and the rest of the class.

Conception

Conception means making a baby. When a man and a woman are in a loving and long-term relationship they may decide to have sex; in other words, they may have sexual intercourse. When a man and a woman express their love for each other by having sex, their bodies react in different ways: the man's penis becomes hard and the woman's vagina becomes wet. This makes it possible for sexual intercourse to take place. During sexual intercourse the man's penis enters the woman's vagina. During intercourse sperm are released into the woman's vagina and travel through her uterus into the Fallopian tubes. If a sperm joins up with an egg in the Fallopian tube, fertilisation occurs. The fertilised egg develops for a few days in the Fallopian tube and then travels to the uterus where it attaches itself to the lining of the uterus. Not all fertilised eggs are implanted in the uterus. If the egg attaches itself to the uterus a baby develops over the next nine months.

Note: in Ireland it is illegal to have sex with anyone under the age of 17. This is called the 'age of consent'.

Some interesting facts

- Sperm can live for up to 5–7 days.
- Only one sperm can penetrate an egg.
- The menstrual cycle of a teenager can be irregular until the body adjusts. Stress, illness and changes in diet or routine can all affect the menstrual cycle.
- When a male is sexually aroused he experiences an erection (this can also happen for no reason at all), which means that the penis becomes hard and expands.
- The release of sperm is called ejaculation.
- Erections do not always result in ejaculation. Sometimes during puberty a boy can ejaculate during his sleep – this is called a wet dream.
- An egg can live for up to 48 hours.
- A woman is born with one million immature eggs in her ovaries.
- Eggs are pushed along the Fallopian tubes by the movement of tiny hairs.
- A female egg is about the size of a full stop.
- The first period is called the menarche.
- On average a woman loses about two and a half tablespoons of blood during her period.
- Some females may become emotional a few days before their period. This is due to changes in hormone levels, and it is known as premenstrual syndrome (PMS) or tension (PMT).

On a piece of paper write down one question or comment about what you have learned today. When you have finished, fold the paper and hand it to your teacher.

Learning *Keepsake*

Three things I have learned about the menstrual cycle and about conception are:

1. _____

2. _____

3. _____

As a result of what I have learned about sexual intercourse and conception, I will:

_____

_____

_____

_____ has shared this Learning Keepsake with me _____

Name of student   Parent's/guardian's signature

LESSON 28

Gender Stereotypes and Discrimination

At the end of this lesson . . .

. . . you will have explored different images of men and women

. . . and have learned about respect for one's own sexuality and the sexuality of others.

Key Words
- Stereotype
- Gender
- Identity

Keyskill
- Working with others

Images of males and females

Drawing conclusions about the way people behave is called stereotyping. For example, 'All teenagers are moody.'

Gender stereotyping means having different expectations of people because they happen to be male or female, e.g. 'Boys don't cry.'

 Individual Activity

Look at the statements below. Tick whether you think they are true, false or sometimes true.

Statement	True?	False?	Sometimes true?
Girls are more sensitive than boys			
Boys are carefree, take risks and don't see the consequences of their actions			
Girls don't want to be seen as intelligent around boys			
Boys act all macho around their male friends			
Girls only want to talk about clothes and make-up			
Boys' main topic of conversation is sport or cars			
Boys should be able to wear make-up			
Boys find it difficult to talk about what's bothering them			
Girls talk about each other behind each other's backs			
Boys are very loyal friends and stick up for each other no matter what			
Girls are more concerned than boys about their appearance			
Girls just like to gossip when they are together			
It is important for boys not to lose face in front of their male friends			
Girls and boys cannot be friends as one of them will always have feelings for the other			
Male sports are more interesting to watch			
A boy should always ask a girl out			
Girls and boys are equal in every way			
Home economics is a girls' subject			
Boys are better suited to technology subjects			

From the table, choose two statements about the opposite gender that you most agree with and say why.

1. a) Statement: _____
    Why you agree: _____

    b) Statement: _____
    Why you agree: _____

2. Where do you think gender stereotypes come from?
    _____
    _____

3. What are the effects of gender stereotyping on males and females in their daily lives?
    _____
    _____

4. Write down other stereotypes in society (e.g. 'All rich people are snobs').
    _____
    _____
    _____

5. How are these people discriminated against?
    _____

Group Activity

How do the women in the photographs support or contradict gender stereotypes?

1. _____
    _____

2. _____
    _____

3. _____
    _____

4. _____
    _____

  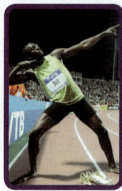 

How do the men in the photographs support or contradict gender stereotypes?

1. _____
_____

2. _____
_____

3. _____
_____

4. _____
_____

Respecting myself and others

Although there have been huge changes in society over the years, male and female stereotyping still exists. Some people still believe that men are suited to certain jobs and women to others. The media try to sell certain images of how men and women should look.

These stereotypes are not healthy and they fail to recognise that every person is unique. It is important to respect your own individuality and the individuality of others. Stereotyping reduces respect for others and excludes people unfairly and can lead to discrimination.

 Pair Activity

Write down one example of gender stereotyping and suggest a way of changing it.
Example: _____

How to change it:

Learning *Keepsake*

Three things I have learned about gender stereotyping are:

1. _____
2. _____
3. _____

As a result of what I have learned about gender stereotyping, I will:

_____

_____

_____

_____ has shared this Learning Keepsake with me _____

Name of student   Parent's/guardian's signature

Topic Review

Date / /

In this topic I learned about

_____

This topic is useful to me in my life because

_____

_____

In this topic I liked

_____

_____

In this topic I did not like

_____

_____

I would like to find out more about

_____

_____

Key Skills I have used in this topic are:

☐ Managing myself

☐ Staying well

☐ Communicating

☐ Being creative

☐ Working with others

☐ Managing information and thinking

*Are you up for the challenge?

Design a wall chart which shows the different talents of students in your class.

Substance Use

LESSON 27

Why Use Drugs?

At the end of this lesson . . .

. . . you will have explored the effects of drug use on health and society

. . . you will have identified why medicine is important in our lives

. . . and you will understand that there are some situations where medicine and drugs are misused.

Key Words
- Prescribed
- Non-prescribed
- Hallucinations

Keyskill
- Staying safe

Group Activity

Brainstorm some of the advances in medicine that have brought benefits to our society over the years.

Drugs

A drug is any substance that changes the way the body works or the way a person thinks, feels or behaves. Drugs are made from chemicals and they work by changing the chemistry of the body. The medicines people take to make them better when they are ill are also drugs. The main types of drugs are:

- **Prescribed medicines** – some legal drugs (antibiotics, for example) can only be given by doctors. These are called 'prescribed drugs', and when you need them your doctor gives you a letter called a prescription to take to your pharmacy.
- **Non-prescribed medicines** can be purchased in a shop, e.g. headache tablets. These are often called over-the-counter medicines.
- **Herbal remedies** are medicines that are considered 'natural' and they can be bought in health food shops.

These drugs are all legal. Other legal drugs include alcohol and tobacco; which are legal, but there are certain legal restrictions around who takes them.
There are also illegal drugs such as cannabis, LSD, cocaine, heroin and ecstasy.

Solvents

Other chemicals which can change the way the body works are solvents. The picture below shows examples of household solvents. Can you name them?

Solvents can be sniffed or sprayed into the mouth or nose. The effects of solvent abuse include:

- feelings of dizziness and excitement
- laughing uncontrollably
- hallucinations (seeing things that are not really there – which can be really frightening)
- nausea and drowsiness
- feeling aggressive
- headaches and nose bleeds.

There have been several tragic deaths from solvent abuse in this country. Solvent use can make the heart beat irregularly, resulting in heart attack. Users can choke on their own vomit or suffocate from their inhalations. Solvent abuse can cause brain, liver, nerve and kidney damage.

Individual Activity

Wordsearch

There are 15 drugs in the word search below. Find them and group them into categories: illegal; prescription; over-the-counter; and herbal.

E	M	P	L	S	D	A	E	H	S	H	C	R	S	S
S	S	B	A	H	T	C	L	X	Y	O	Z	E	A	M
I	O	O	H	R	S	N	E	C	D	L	N	X	N	O
B	N	Y	R	T	A	N	E	L	O	I	B	N	T	O
A	U	I	A	M	I	C	I	V	C	H	I	D	I	R
N	N	S	O	T	I	V	E	I	L	D	O	R	B	H
N	Y	E	O	R	E	R	D	T	A	O	P	L	I	S
A	S	C	S	R	E	E	P	N	A	K	S	C	O	U
C	I	B	O	K	M	H	A	G	K	M	C	H	T	M
N	I	I	Z	H	M	R	M	U	N	W	O	Q	I	C
M	L	H	G	V	M	F	P	O	N	I	M	L	C	I
W	X	U	C	A	F	F	E	I	N	E	N	M	S	G
B	O	S	L	L	I	P	T	E	I	D	I	E	I	A
C	X	W	P	K	F	E	N	I	A	C	O	C	V	M
H	E	R	B	A	L	T	A	B	L	E	T	S	S	E

solvents, cannabis, magic mushrooms, nicotine, diet pills, alcohol, caffeine, ecstasy, heroin, cocaine, herbal tablets, paracetamol, antibiotics, LSD, cough medicines, Anadin, evening primrose, cod liver oil.

Illegal	Prescription	Over-the-counter	Herbal

Drug misuse

Drug misuse includes:

1. using illegal drugs
2. taking legal drugs (e.g. alcohol, tobacco) before the legal age
3. using legal drugs incorrectly
4. solvent abuse.

The effects of drug misuse include:

- damage to relationships
- violence
- loss of self-control
- health issues
- breaking the law.

Design a poster listing the dangers of drug misuse. Use slogans, pictures and bright colours to make your poster eye-catching.

Learning *Keepsake*

Three things I have learned about drugs are:

1. _____
2. _____
3. _____

As a result of what I have learned about drugs, I will:

_____

_____

_____

_____ has shared this Learning Keepsake with me _____

Name of student   Parent's/guardian's signature

LESSON 30

Smoking and its Effects

At the end of this lesson . . .
. . . you will have considered the health and social effects of smoking.

Key Words
- Cardiovascular disease

Keyskill
- Staying safe

Individual Activity

Read the following article from a popular teenage magazine and answer the questions that follow.

Think Smoking is Cool?

The truth of the matter is smoking is stupid. Plain and simple.

When you think of the physical action of what you are doing, it's pretty foul. You are taking smoky air into your lungs and then exhaling it. And this is meant to be fun? Would you run a tube up a smoky chimney and do the same? Would you stand right behind a bus and inhale the fumes? Uh, no!

It's not like anyone sets out to be a smoker. Sometimes it's boredom, sometimes it's because the guy you like is a smoker, sometimes it's because all your friends are doing it. However, before you know what's happening you're not just taking a cigarette from someone else, you're buying a packet, then another. Now it's not just when you're with your mates, it's when your parents aren't home or when you're babysitting and you have a cheeky puff out the window.

A smoker is someone who smokes and it doesn't have to be twenty a day. And being called a smoker is no compliment.

How does it affect how I look?

Before we even get started on the health risk, there are other smoking concerns to consider. Your looks, for example. For a start your teeth will turn from their previous bright and shiny whiteness to a dull beige and eventually develop brown stains starting at the gums.

Attractive! And not only does it look like a mouthful of rotting teeth, boy does it make your breath pong. And we are not talking smoky stinky, we're talking actual bad breath. You're getting ready to go out, maybe you're meeting your mates. You start by having a long bath before spraying on your favourite perfume or aftershave. You smell gorgeous! You brush your teeth to a dazzling white and head out the door. Then you light up a cigarette and ruin everything. You may as well have washed your hair in sour milk, rolled around in manure and eaten a round of garlic bread because after a cigarette you're going to stink anyway. Hair, clothes, fingers . . . why even bother washing at all when you are going to smell so wrong?!

And if stinking to high heavens is not bad enough, smoking actually causes premature ageing of the skin too. Though you may feel that this is no cause for concern right now, you will soon know all about it. Not only will it give you rotten wrinkles around the eyes and the forehead, you'll also get attractive wrinkles around your mouth. So while your non-smoking mates are enjoying getting ID'd by club bouncers at the age of 28 ('Really? I look underage?' they'll grin), you're getting asked for your pensioner's travel pass on the bus: not good.

'What about my health?'

If brown teeth, stinky breath and premature wrinkles aren't enough to put you off smoking, then maybe the fact that ninety per cent of lung cancers are caused by smoking will convince you.

Not to mention the fact that your life will be shortened by ten to fifteen years.

Individual Activity

1. 'Although young people are informed about the effects of smoking they still do not regard it as dangerous.' Do you agree with this statement? Give reasons for your answer.

    _____

    _____

2. If you were trying to reduce smoking among young people in Ireland what three facts about smoking would you consider the most important?

    a) _____

    b) _____

    c) _____

3. What is your school's policy on smoking?

    _____

    _____

4. What do you think when you see smoking advertisements opposite? Do you think they influence a person's decision to smoke?

    _____

    _____

   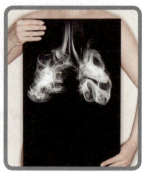

What's in a cigarette?

What causes the damage?

There are some really gross 'ingredients' in fags that will make you very sick.

Nicotine. This is what gets people hooked on cigarettes, as it's a highly addictive chemical. It's so toxic it was also used in the past as a greenhouse insecticide.

Tar. An oily brown substance found in tobacco leaves that's inhaled when you smoke. It builds up in the lungs, causing cancer.

Carbon monoxide. Yes, the same gas that's emitted from car exhausts and that causes smog is in cigarettes. It's a poisonous gas and when inhaled it damages the way your heart and blood vessels work.

What about passive smoking?

Passive smoking means breathing in the smoke in the air; this is known as ETS or Environmental Tobacco Smoke. If your mates or family smoke they are not just harming their own health, they're damaging yours too. It's not just the smoke we can see and smell that is damaging, it's the invisible gases too. ETS causes lung cancer and heart disease in non-smokers.

You probably find if you're sitting in a room where people are smoking that you experience a sore throat, itchy, runny eyes, coughing, sneezing and headache. It may also make you feel nauseous, dizzy or even cause respiratory problems such as bronchitis or pneumonia.

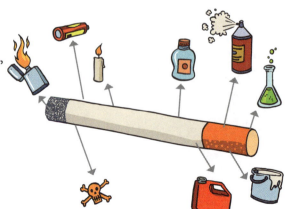

Ingredient:		Also used as/in:
Arsenic		Rat poison
Ammonia		Cleaning product/bleach
Cyanide		Deadly poison
Acetone		Nail polish remover
Butane		Lighter fluid
DDT		Insecticide
Sulphuric acid		Car batteries
Cadmium		Batteries (toxic metal)
Preon		Gas in fridges
Methoprene		Pesticide

Some facts about smoking

- Cigarette smoke contains 4,000 chemicals.
- Smoking is the single biggest killer of people in Ireland: tobacco kills more people each year than car crashes, illegal drugs and Aids combined.
- 12 per cent of children aged between 10 and 18 in Ireland say they currently smoke.
- Smoking does not relax you – it triggers stress.
- Smoking affects sports performance because the carbon monoxide in cigarettes deprives the muscles of oxygen.
- Most smokers will lose between 10 and 15 quality life years before they die.
- 1 in 2 smokers will die from a tobacco-related illness such as cancer, heart disease, lung disease, cardiovascular disease and exacerbation of diabetes.
- Smoking accounts for some 5,500 deaths in Ireland each year.
- Smoking 20 cigarettes a day could cost a person over €3,000 a year.
- The benefits of quitting smoking are felt almost immediately by the body.
- One cigar can contain as much tobacco as a pack of cigarettes.
- It is illegal for anyone under the age of 18 to buy cigarettes in Ireland.
- Young people whose friends smoke are more likely to start.
- It takes 20 minutes for a smoker's pulse rate to return to normal after having a cigarette.

Two facts that surprised me most about smoking are

1. _____

2. _____

Crossword

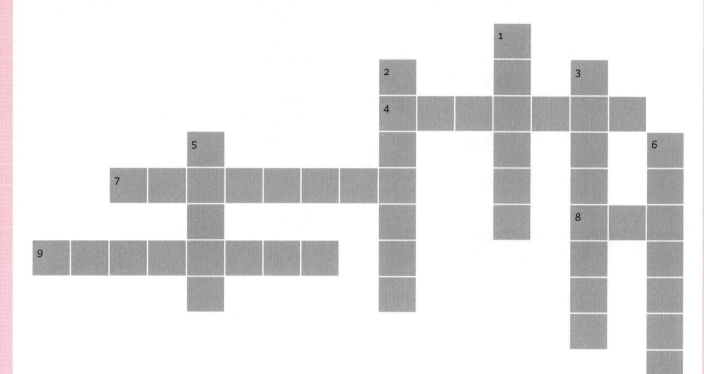

Across

4   One of the 4,000 chemicals in cigarettes, often used as rat poison.
7   Visible signs of premature ageing.
8   In a smoker this builds up in the lungs, making it hard to breath.
9   This will reduce your chances of getting a smoking-related illness.

Down

1   It takes this many minutes for a smoker's heart rate to return to normal after smoking a cigarette.
2   This type of smoking harms non-smokers.
3   This makes cigarettes highly addictive.
5   Out of 100 people who smoke, this many people will die of a tobacco-related illness.
6   This gas robs the body of oxygen and causes shortness of breath.

Learning *Keepsake*

Three things I have learned about smoking are:

1. _____

2. _____

3. _____

As a result of what I have learned about smoking, I will:

_____

_____

_____

_____ has shared this Learning Keepsake with me _____

Name of student   Parent's/guardian's signature

LESSON 31

Alcohol: the facts

At the end of this lesson you will . . .
. . . you will understand how alcohol affects personal health and relationships.

Key Words
- Standard drink
- Alcohol limit

Keyskill
- Staying safe

Below are some pictures of situations in which people use alcohol. Look at the pictures and answer the questions in the spaces provided.

1. Why do you think alcohol is being used in this situation?
2. What risks could be associated with drinking alcohol in this situation?
3. How can these risks be avoided?

1. _____
2. _____
3. _____

1. _____
2. _____
3. _____

1. _____
2. _____
3. _____

1. _____
2. _____
3. _____

1. _____
2. _____
3. _____

1. _____
2. _____
3. _____

1. _____
2. _____
3. _____

1. _____
2. _____
3. _____

Suggest some other situations in which drinking alcohol can lead to problems.

How alcohol affects different parts of the body

The moment alcohol enters your body it starts affecting your body and mind. Alcohol passes through the body from the mouth, to the stomach, into the circulatory system, the brain, the kidneys, lungs and liver. As alcohol is consumed the following can occur.

Brain

Alcohol affects the part of the brain that is responsible for self-control. As a person drinks, their reactions, vision and judgement become impaired. The more a person drinks, the harder basic tasks – such as walking and talking – become. After drinking, people sometimes say and do things they don't mean and behave out of character. An excessive amount of alcohol in the body can result in coma, brain damage and even death.

Stomach

Alcohol passes through the walls of the stomach and small intestines into the bloodstream. If the stomach is empty the alcohol passes straight through; if the stomach has food in it the alcohol is absorbed more slowly. Alcohol stimulates the stomach juices, which causes an increase in appetite.

Circulatory system

Once it is in the bloodstream alcohol is distributed around the body. Alcohol widens the blood vessels as it goes through the bloodstream and this can account for flushed skin and feelings of warmth.

Lungs

Alcohol in its gaseous state is inhaled into the bloodstream and goes straight to the lungs.

Kidneys

Alcohol stimulates urine production, which causes a person to urinate more. This leads to dehydration.

Liver

90% of alcohol is broken down by the liver, but the liver can only deal with one drink per hour. Alcohol damages the liver when it is consumed regularly.

Skin

Drinking alcohol dehydrates the skin, causing bloating and dark circles under the eyes.

Did you know?

Drinking alcohol can cause weight gain. Drinking one pint of beer is equivalent to eating a hamburger.

Fill in other possible problems associated with alcohol use

Legal problems	Suspended driver's licence Fines Imprisonment
Family problems	
Financial problems	
School problems	
Personal problems	

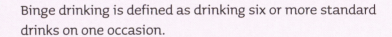

Binge drinking is defined as drinking six or more standard drinks on one occasion.

Individual Activity

You are trying to raise awareness of the risks of alcohol use among young people in Ireland. Design a T-shirt highlighting the most important piece of information you would like to get across.

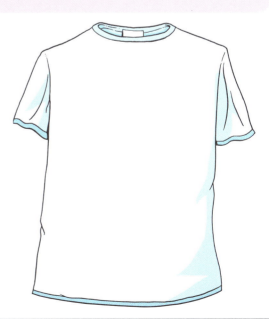

Learning *Keepsake*

Three things I have learned about alcohol are:

1. _____
2. _____
3. _____

As a result of what I have learned about alcohol, I will:

_____
_____
_____

_____ has shared this Learning Keepsake with me _____
Name of student   Parent's/guardian's signature

Topic Review

Date   /   /

In this topic I learned about

_____

This topic is useful to me in my life because

_____

_____

In this topic I liked

_____

_____

In this topic I did not like

_____

_____

I would like to find out more about

_____

_____

Key Skills I have used in this topic are:

- ☐ Managing myself
- ☐ Staying well
- ☐ Communicating
- ☐ Being creative
- ☐ Working with others
- ☐ Managing information and thinking

*Are you up for the challenge?

Your class are going to lead a campaign to highlight the risks of smoking or drinking alcohol. As part of the campaign your group must create a poem or a piece of rap music on the effects of smoking or alcohol.

Acknowledgements

The authors and publisher are grateful to the following for permission to reproduce copyrighted material:

Adapted information on physical activity guidelines from www.getirelandactive.ie

'The Wind Beneath My Wings' words and music by Jeff Silbar and Larry Henley (c) 1982 WB Music Corp. (ASCAP) and Warner-Tamerlane Publishing Corp. (BMI)

The authors and publisher have made every effort to trace all copyright holders, but if any has been inadvertently overlooked we would be pleased to make the necessary arrangement at the first opportunity.